DISENTANGLE YOUR ANXIETY

An Introductory Anxiety Book on Identifying, Understanding, and Overcoming Your Anxious Symptoms Before They Take Over Your Life

Marie French

© Copyright 2022 - All rights reserved. The contents of this book may not be reproduced, duplicated or transmitted without direct written permission from the author. Under no circumstances will any legal responsibility or blame be held against the publisher for any reparation, damages, or monetary loss due to the information herein, either directly or indirectly.

Legal Notice: This book is copyright protected. This is only for personal use. You cannot amend, distribute, sell, use, quote or paraphrase any part or the content within this book without the consent of the author.

Disclaimer Notice: Please note the information contained within this document is for educational and entertainment purposes only. Every attempt has been made to provide accurate, up to date and reliable complete information. No warranties of any kind are expressed or implied. Readers acknowledge that the author is not engaging in the rendering of legal, financial, medical or professional advice. The content of this book has been derived from various sources. Please consult a licensed professional before attempting any techniques outlined in this book. By reading this document, the reader agrees that under no circumstances is the author responsible for any losses, direct or indirect, which are incurred as a result of the use of information contained within this document, including, but not limited to, errors, omissions, or inaccuracies.

Author Bio

Marie French has dedicated her life to helping those who suffer from anxiety and need to get their life back on track. She helps increase awareness, knowledge, and understanding of the early signs of anxiety, to prevent it from escalating, and believes everyone can learn to manage their symptoms, but they must first learn to understand it.

As an anxiety sufferer from an early age herself, she knows just how bad anxiety can get if left untreated and is able to draw on her own unique experiences over the last 25 years, to help others get to grips with her anxiety.

Anxiety has always had a role in her life, and even her career was built on this. As well as supporting many adults, she was also able to help her son, who suffered from anxiety symptoms in childhood. This book is designed to help you in the same way.

Table of Contents

Introduction 1

Chapter 1: Anxiety Interferes with Your Potential 9

Chapter 2: Defining Feelings and Symptoms
of Anxiety.. 15

    Different Types of Anxiety 16

    Anxiety, Stress, and Nervousness –
    Let's Get Clear 17

    Who is at Risk of Anxiety Disorders? 19

    Anxiety Myths 19

Chapter 3: Accept Who You Are................................... 23

    What is Self-Acceptance and Why is
    it Important? 24

    5 Steps to Self-Acceptance 25

    Self-Acceptance Activities 28

Chapter 4: Know Your Triggers................................... 31

    9 Common Anxiety Triggers 31

    Why is it Important to Know My Triggers? 34

    How Can Knowing My Triggers Help Me Avoid or
    Prevent Anxiety Symptoms? 35

Chapter 5: Research the Enemy 39
What Kind of Research Should I Do When it Comes to My Anxiety? 40
Why is it Important to Understand What Makes Me Feel Anxious? 43
How Can Researching My Anxiety Help Me Overcome it? 45

Chapter 6: Plan of Attack 49
What Should I Do After Accepting Myself, Identifying My Triggers, and Researching the Anxiety? 50
Why is it Important to Plan Accordingly? 55
How Can Planning the Right Action Help Me Overcome Anxiety? 56

Chapter 7: Mind, Body, and Spirit 59
What is the First Thing to Manage When Trying to Prevent Anxiety? 59
Why is it Important to Consider My Well-being? 64
How Can I Begin to Incorporate a Healthier Lifestyle? 66

Chapter 8: Become a Planner 69
What Kind of Planning Should I Be Doing? 70
Why is Planning Beneficial? 72
How Can I Begin to Be More Plan-Oriented With My Life? 73

Chapter 9: Take Time for Yourself 77
What Kind of Things Should I Take Time to Do for Myself? 78

Why is it Important That I Have Me Time? 81
How Can I Fit Me Time Into My Busy Life? 83

Chapter 10: It's All About Perspective 85
What Does "It's All About Perspective" Mean? 86
Why is the Way I Perceive Life Important? 87
How Can This Ultimately Reduce My Anxiety? 88
Activity 90

Chapter 11: Facing Anxiety from Responsibility 93
What is Hypengyophobia? 94
Why is it Important to Conquer this Fear? 95
How Can I Begin to Overcome Hypengyophobia? ... 97

Chapter 12: Facing Anxiety in Relationships 101
What is Relationship Anxiety? 101
Why is it Important to Deal With This? 104
How Can I Practice Overcoming
Relationship Anxiety? 106

Chapter 13: Facing Anxiety When Speaking 111
What Do I Do if I Become Anxious and
Have to Speak? 112
Why is it Important to Crush This Fear? 113
How Can I Become a Better Speaker and
Remove This Anxiety? 114

Chapter 14: Facing Anxiety from Everyday Life 119
What Kind of Anxiety Comes in Everyday Life? 119
Why is This Form of Anxiety Important to
Overcome? 122

How Can I Be Prepared for Anxious
Moments in My Life?...................................122

Chapter 15: It's Not About Control; It's About Commitment.. 129
You're Doing Great!......................................132

Chapter 16: Anxiety Can Lead to Deception 135
What if I Fall Into Bad Habits?....................136
What if I Don't Think I'm Good Enough? 138
What if I Don't Have a Purpose to Aim for? 139

Chapter 17: Anxiety isn't Always a Bad Thing! 143
What Does Anxiety Mean to You? 144
Why is it Important to See Anxiety as a
Good Thing?...145
How Can I Begin to Look at Anxiety in a
New Light?... 147

Chapter 18: Where to Find Relief................................ 151
What Can Others Do to Help with Anxiety?...........152
Why is it Important to Have the Support
of Others?...155
How Can Others Make a Difference in
My Growth?...157

Chapter 19: Anxiety-Free Living................................. 161
Your Perfect Day...163
Your Progress With Anxiety 164
But... I'm Not Quite There Yet 165
Your Future is in Your Hands......................165

Chapter 20: Intentionally Reaching Goals And Changing Others **169**

    Review 169

    How Can I Stay Intentional When it Comes to
Achieving My Goals? 175

    Carter the Worrier 176

References List **179**

Introduction

Anxiety is difficult to describe because unless you've experienced it, you don't really understand its impact. It's a big, personal knot that you need to unravel, as everyone experiences anxiety differently. There are various symptoms of anxiety, but if it's not recognized and dealt with early on, the knot just gets bigger and more tangled because it doesn't take anxiety long to turn into a big mess.

Anxiety is that feeling of unease or dread, which can result in you feeling nauseous, tense, unable to move, or shaky; it can even make your heart race. Symptoms are hugely linked to worry and fear, and it can start off very mild at first, so mild that you don't even notice it's becoming a problem. Most people experience anxiety throughout their life, but they don't always recognize what it is. Many people cope with feelings of anxiety well as it's in our nature to cope, but for others, the feelings fester and worsen. Before we know it, they've taken hold of us. It's incapacitating. That's anxiety.

> *"Anxiety is a thin stream of fear trickling through the mind. If encouraged, it cuts a channel into which all other thoughts are drained."*
>
> ~ Arthur Somers Roche

Anxiety can change our life as we know it, because it limits the things we can do. The good news is that anxiety is something we can learn to understand and overcome. So, like me, if you're tired of anxious symptoms that have been haunting you, it's time to beat them and regain control.

The first time I noticed how my anxiety symptoms were making life difficult was when I was studying for an exam in college. I had been extremely calm until the time for the exam arrived and I entered the hall. My heart was racing, I could hear my breathing loudly, and I was fidgeting. When the hall fell silent, I felt clammy, and it took a while for me to start writing my paper because I was too distracted by my surroundings and overwhelmed by my feelings. Following this, I noticed this happening more and more, and each episode got more intense. Going for job interviews, shopping, and family or work events, all started to become a strain until I dreaded leaving the house. Everything was hard and I felt helpless. It wasn't just a feeling; I was physically incapacitated as my body didn't want to work as it should. Everything was an effort.

I vowed to myself that I wasn't going to let my anxiety symptoms escalate and control my life...

I started to learn more about anxiety and got to understand it and how it impacted me. By using some simple, but tried and tested methods, and by working on

Introduction

myself, I was able to turn my life around. Now, anxiety no longer stands in my way because I have it under control.

If you:

- Want to stop getting stressed out over tiny, unimportant things
- Are ready to combat those debilitating symptoms caused by anxiety
- Are eager to take a deep dive into anxiety
- Understand that the path to overcoming anxiety is a journey of self-discovery
- Want to embrace your life by freeing yourself of fear and worry

Then you're ready for this book!

This book explores how anxiety interferes with your life and your potential. We'll talk through some key strategies as we explore your own personal pathway to overcoming your anxiety. By exploring anxiety symptoms, you'll be able to get to the root cause and understand what makes you tick. You'll learn to accept yourself for who you are and consider what triggers you as you evaluate your own anxiety and formulate your plan of attack. As we move into the next section of the book, you'll discuss strategies to help you get your symptoms under control, and you'll learn how to take time for yourself, along with some important skills to help you put the most important things into perspective.

As the focus shifts to overcoming your anxiety in Section 3 of this book, you'll also consider how you can conquer your anxiety and take responsibility for it. You'll then get to look at different scenarios regarding anxiety, for example how you can face anxiety symptoms in your relationships when speaking and dealing with them in your everyday life. Disentangling anxiety is about committing to yourself and your own needs, so you can learn to use anxiety for the greater good.

With the knowledge and strategies uncovered in this book, you'll fulfill your ultimate goal by living your life free from the restraints that anxiety place on you. We're ready to show you how!

Over time, symptoms of anxiety can impact your physical and mental health, which means it's vital to get it under control. It's one of the most common forms of mental illness, so preventing this from escalating can stop you from having more severe episodes later. A person who has suffered with more severe forms of anxiety understands what it's like to be anxious, but this can leave them feeling lonely. It's important to understand that you are not alone in this battle. It's believed that approximately 275 million people in the world suffer from anxiety disorders, and that's not even counting the majority of people who suffer with anxiety without a diagnosed condition.

There are so many benefits of disentangling your anxiety. For example, you're more likely to have sensitive and loving relationships, you're happier and more confident, and you take control of your life. Your body will automatically flag-up symptoms of anxiety and fight against it to prevent a negative outcome. People who overcome their anxious symptoms are often more motivated, alert, and positive, so you'll be ready and willing to take on whatever life throws at you.

Introduction

When we talk about disentangling your anxiety, it's quite a broad term, but to put this simply, it's making you aware that you'll naturally increase your awareness to your triggers, which means you'll learn to manage your symptoms and, therefore, you can minimize the impact they have on you. By being able to overcome the paralysis caused by anxiety, you're free to live your life and strive for the things you really want.

Anxiety is serious! I suffered from anxiety for many years, and it got to the point where anxiety controlled my life. Everything I did from making new connections and forming relationships to learning, working, and my social life were limited by anxiety. Anxiety wasn't something that came on suddenly. It crept up on me over time and beat me down bit by bit. I didn't even know I was anxious at first, all I knew was that I was constantly worried, isolated, and didn't know why, and neither did my family and friends. It took a long time to get a diagnosis, but if I had recognized the early signs and symptoms of anxiety, things may have been different.

Anxiety started to impact my physical health, so I visited my doctor—convinced that I had a life-threatening illness—but after a few tests and a good check-over, it was suggested that I was suffering from anxiety, which was impacting both my mental and physical health. He provided me with some information and signposted me to a therapist who helped me strengthen my understanding of anxiety. With this diagnosis, everything began to make sense; however, it took a long time to work through the issues, because while I could accept that I had anxiety, I had no idea what had caused this.

Getting to the root cause of my anxiety was a challenge because it had been going on much longer than I initially thought, and I soon became obsessed and researched more and more. I attended courses on CBT topics, mindfulness and meditation, and started to attend a yoga class. Although the journey was long, it was a pleasure, and now I help others to come to grips with and overcome their anxiousness by raising awareness of the most common symptoms. I do this because I believe we can disentangle from anxiety together. I also recognized the signs of anxiety in my son, who suffered from attachment issues, at a young age. Getting the early help he needed made a huge difference in his life for the better.

It's my life's mission to support others who suffer from anxiety symptoms before they escalate by raising awareness, knowledge, and understanding the early signs of anxiety.

The skills and strategies you adopt by reading this book equips you for life, so you can continuously rally against those feelings of anxiousness. In fact, you'll be able to reason with how you feel and deal with it, before any problems escalate as you'll recognize the early signs.

Anxiety isn't something to be ignored...

> *"Anxiety does not empty tomorrow of its sorrows, but only empties today of its strength."*
>
> *~ Charles Spurgeon*

This is not simply a book that instructs you on what to do, it holds you accountable and demands that you take action and deal with any debilitating symptoms you face.

Introduction

It's a new way of living your life; staying present in the now and allowing yourself to pull back and reason with your negative thought patterns before they take hold.

If you're ready to begin your incredible journey to disentangling your anxiety before its symptoms take over your life, head over to Chapter 1 to learn more about anxiety symptoms and how they sabotage your life and your potential.

Let's do this together!

Chapter 1

Anxiety Interferes with Your Potential

It's true! Anxiety interferes with your potential, but have you ever wondered…

Why do we allow this?

You can prevent this from happening, you just need to feel empowered enough to do this, and we're going to show you how.

If anxiety has already taken hold of you, it's likely you already feel like it has, or you may even believe that you don't have potential (but that's not true).

But at what point do your anxiety symptoms interfere with your potential?

Everyone feels anxious from time to time, but typically, it's mild and passes reasonably quickly. Someone may have feelings of worry or anxiousness about a job interview, for example, this would pass once the interview is over. While this doesn't mean you have an anxiety disorder, such a feeling may be a symptom of anxiousness. This type of anxiousness or nervousness is normal, however, while some people only have mild anxiety, others suffer more severely and develop an anxiety disorder. This is because their anxiety gets out of control.

Anxiety interferes with your potential when it starts to limit your life and prevents you from doing the things you want to do. We all have dreams, and long lists of things we want to do, but unless we're able to consistently work toward those things, we're never going to achieve them. If you're experiencing symptoms of anxiety, it can hold you back and stop you from striving forward and progressing in life. This means you stagnate.

When your anxiety symptoms escalate, you can become irrational. You may find that you withdraw from friends and family and begin a journey of self-destruction. The deeper we get, the more difficult it is to remedy, and we may start to see social situations as a threat. This isn't the path you should go down if you can help it; we don't want that for you. This book helps you to delve deep into your early symptoms of anxiety, so you can identify and overcome any symptoms you have; this way, you can prevent this type of escalation and meet your potential.

If your symptoms of anxiety intensify, you could develop anxiety. Anxiety is a condition that impacts your mental health, especially if it goes unrecognized. It can lead to an anxiety disorder, but it can also be a sign of other mental health issues. For example, when anxiety grows, it can cause stress, depression, and even self-harm. Things like this aren't talked about enough, as many people find it uncomfortable to talk about how they feel. This is something this book hopes to change, and this change starts with you.

There are several types of anxiety disorders, and it's important that you're aware of these. This book is an introduction and focuses on identifying and overcoming early anxiety symptoms, but if you think you may suffer from an anxiety disorder, you must speak to your doctor, as you need specialist support and a diagnosis. Types of anxiety disorders include:

- Panic disorder
- Separation anxiety disorder
- Social anxiety disorder
- Agoraphobia and other phobias
- Generalized anxiety disorder
- Selective mutism
- Anxiety disorder due to another health condition

This book cannot help you diagnose anxiety but can help you recognize feelings of anxiousness and increase your understanding. You should see your doctor if you feel overcome with fear or worry and this is beginning to upset you, if you believe your anxious feelings are difficult to control, if you feel depressed, or have started using drugs or alcohol to help you cope, if you have other mental health concerns or if you believe your anxiety is linked to a physical health problem, if you feel like your anxiety is interfering with parts of your life, such as your relationships or work, or if you have suicidal thoughts or indulge in behaviors that put you at risk.

When a person starts suffering from more severe forms of anxiety, they begin to blow things out of proportion, so a fairly small problem is amplified. It can be very overwhelming, and it can destroy their happiness. It can cause you real distress, which is why it's extremely important to learn how to recognize the signs and cope, before it prevents you from meeting your potential. Sometimes, those who are prone to anxiety experience a traumatic event, a build-up of stress, or for those who have blood relatives with an anxiety disorder, an anxiety disorder can be triggered. With that in mind, seeking advice from a medical professional is extremely important, as you should never suffer in silence.

When I noticed anxiety had become a problem for me, I didn't know how to get help. For some people, symptoms begin in childhood or during their teenage years. For others, it develops in adulthood. It doesn't discriminate by age. At first, I didn't even realize that I had anxiety and when I did, I thought it would pass because I honestly didn't think it would become a problem.

There was a time when anxiety became debilitating, and I felt completely out of control. I'd have trouble sleeping, eating, and I'd constantly feel like I was on edge. I've even had gastrointestinal problems, and headaches, and I've felt extremely weak. I didn't even know they were symptoms, but I did know this couldn't continue.

The therapist my doctor referred me to was a valuable form of support and was able to suggest some different techniques to help with the anxiety, which is what started me off on my journey of self-discovery. This proved to be the key to overcoming my anxiety as I learned to identify my triggers, accept who I am, and take action to make improvements in my life.

Learning to cope with my anxiety symptoms has changed my life for the better—because it's allowed—and I know this book can have a positive impact on your life too. No longer do I need to bury my head in the sand and allow my feelings to overwhelm me so much that I feel unable to move or act. I now have the life I want, and it even helped me form stronger relationships in my life, while also improving my career. I'm fulfilled and happy!

I am now able to look at the bigger picture, make time for worries, and now I understand my anxiety symptoms on a whole new level. I use the strategies I've learned automatically, which have allowed me to shift my focus, work through the anxiousness by challenging myself, and moving beyond it. Your anxiety symptoms are limiting your life and, therefore, they're interfering with your potential. But you have the power to change that.

Let me just leave this quote here for you:

> *"Life is ten percent what you experience and ninety percent how you respond to it."*
>
> ~ Dorothy M. Neddermeyer

This book is all about increasing your awareness of anxiety, so you can identify the signs and symptoms that impact you. While your anxious symptoms can interfere with your potential, we're not going to let that happen. We're going to disentangle it, so you can live the life you want and deserve!

In the next chapter, we're about to delve deeper into anxiety and its symptoms. While you already have an idea of this, we're going to make it really clear for you. We'll also discuss why it's so important to know what anxiety is. The knowledge provided here will form the foundations for an anxiety-free life. You don't have to do this alone, so let's embark on this journey together.

Chapter 2

Defining Feelings and Symptoms of Anxiety

Many people hear the term anxiety, but it's sometimes difficult to determine what exactly it means. *But if we don't know what it means, how do we even know if we suffer from anxiety or not?*

Let's just clarify that when we refer to anxiety in this book, we are referring to the symptoms of early anxiety, when your anxiety symptoms are becoming a problem as they are beginning to escalate but are not part of a diagnosed condition or anxiety disorder. Such conditions can only be diagnosed and treated by a specialist doctor. The term anxiety is linked to other feelings we experience, such as stress, fear, worry, or nervousness, which is why it's more important than ever to understand what this is. Such feelings can be symptoms of anxiety, but not in every case. There are also anxiety disorders to consider, which are different from anxiety itself as they are actually diagnosed conditions. If we are able to clearly define anxiety, we can learn to come to terms with the symptoms we have and can therefore begin to battle our anxiety.

According to Anxiety.org, common anxiety is '...*the mind and body's reaction to stressful, dangerous, or unfamiliar situations.*' We've all experienced that feeling of distress, unease, or dread, when we know something is about to happen, or has happened—this is an indicator of anxiety. Sometimes, the feeling is in the pit of your stomach, increases your heartbeat, or it causes you to feel sick at the thought of performing an action. It's the thing inside us that makes us stop and doubt ourselves, even if it's just for a minute, but we do.

When you know what anxiety is for you, you can begin to unpack it, and work out your triggers. Only then will you be able to work on overcoming the barriers you face, in light of your anxiousness.

Different Types of Anxiety

Most people cope well with anxiety, in fact, anxiety sometimes encourages us, makes us more determined, or helps us to focus. But some people develop anxiety disorders which are much more debilitating.

If a person has an anxiety disorder or suffers regularly from anxiety, it can prevent them from getting on with their lives. With an anxiety disorder, the feelings of anxiety don't go away and even get worse. This can impact the relationships in your life, your education, and your performance at work.

There are several types of anxiety disorders, which includes generalized anxiety disorder (GAD), panic disorder, and phobias. A GAD is when people worry excessively about every day, ordinary issues such as money, health, family, or work. This becomes GAD when the anxiety occurs almost every day for at least six months.

A panic disorder is when people have sudden periods of intense fear, when there is actually nothing to worry about. They are referred to as panic attacks, and can come on quickly, lasting several minutes. Phobias are when people are uncontrollable intensely frightened about something in particular that poses very little or no danger. There are named phobias referring to enclosed spaces, spiders, open spaces, crowded places, flying, and even social situations.

Anxiety, Stress, and Nervousness – Let's Get Clear

Even though they are similar, there are some differences between anxiety, stress, and nervousness, as it is your body's response to a difficult situation. Stress and nervousness can trigger anxiety, but they are also symptoms of it. That's why it's so important to recognize the symptoms of these things too, as they could lead to anxiety in the future, if they escalate.

If you are nervous, you could:

- Feel exhausted
- Tremble or shake
- Have difficulty focusing or remembering things
- Even feel nauseous

People sometimes believe that nervousness and stress are the same as anxiety, but that's not true. Nervousness goes away after a while, but stress is an emotional strain due to the circumstances we face.

A person who is stressed may:

- Procrastinate
- Put things off that they could do now
- Lie awake worrying at night
- Be easily frustrated
- Grind their teeth
- Have sweaty hands
- Have dry mouth
- Have a pounding heart

There are different forms of anxiety, and it can have crippling effects. If a person is anxious and thinks they could have an anxiety disorder, they may:

- Have a range of physical symptoms, such as:
    - Shortness of breath
    - Unexplained aches and pains
    - Rapid heartbeat
    - Dizziness
- Suffer from anxious thoughts or beliefs that they struggle to control. This usually means they impact daily life, and do not improve on their own
- Experience changes in behavior, such as avoiding activities you previously enjoyed
- Feel stressed (or experience symptoms of stress)
- Be nervous (or suffer from symptoms of nervousness)

It's also worth noting that certain medicines, substances, and caffeine, can all worsen the situation.

You can therefore see how anxiety is different from both stress and nervousness, even though they have some similarities and present some similar symptoms. Stress, nervousness, and anxiety can all be debilitating. All three conditions have this in common.

Who is at Risk of Anxiety Disorders?

There are some people who are at a higher risk of anxiety disorders than others, so in order to increase your awareness, you need to know about this. This includes people who have experienced trauma in their early childhood or adulthood, those with a family history of mental disorders, including anxiety, and those with certain physical health conditions like arrhythmia or thyroid issues. People who are shy or withdrawn when they first meet new people or find themselves in new situations are also at risk.

Just because a person is at risk, doesn't mean they will certainly have an anxiety disorder. There are also treatments that help you deal with your anxiety in a much more effective way, such as CBT, or occasionally, medication, if your healthcare professional sees fit.

It's down to a doctor, psychologist, psychiatrist, or any other medical profession who specializes in anxiety, to diagnose you with an anxiety disorder, but this can take time. They will first need to discuss your symptoms, medical history, and in some cases, they perform tests to get to the root cause.

Anxiety Myths

1. Anxiety is embarrassing

This is a really common myth as so many people find themselves feeling alone when it comes to anxiety, but anxiety is more common than you think. Over 40 million American adults suffer from anxiety.

2. Anxiety isn't a real illness

While diagnosing anxiety could be tricky as it isn't an illness you can do a blood test for, it is a known, diagnosable, medical illness. It, therefore, is an illness, but it can be managed well if the patient is provided with the right tools

3. Anxiety just means you worry

While anxiety does involve worry, it's the way that the worrying impacts you, debilitates you, and stops you living your normal, daily life. Even conditions such as obsessive-compulsive disorder are a type of anxiety disorder, but this is a diagnosed condition that is treated by a doctor. Anxiety is much more than worry, it's complicated, and it can be out of control before you realize it.

Now that you've defined anxiety and its symptoms, you're starting to build a better understanding of its impact. When we feel anxious or have anxiety, it's different for everyone, so it's essential that you get to know yourself and recognize what anxiety means for you. In the next section, you're going to learn how to assess and evaluate your own anxiety, and you'll be able to use this knowledge to overcome your symptoms before they take over your life.

It's time to start disentangling!

Section 1: Evaluating your Anxiety

Chapter 3

Accept Who You Are

Acceptance is a powerful tool that many people don't tap into. Human beings are renowned for their uniqueness, but for many, it's difficult to be comfortable in who we are. Self-acceptance can help you lead a happier, healthier, and peaceful life, but answer this question for me...

Do you regularly check in with yourself to find out how you're doing and assess the things you really want in life?

You see, knowing yourself well is the key to happiness, and yet, many of us don't really know ourselves as we don't take the time to find out, so we put our own needs and wants aside. We try to conform to being the person who we think we ought to be, or that other people think we should be, rather than being true to ourselves.

One of the first steps to overcoming anxiety is self-acceptance. It allows you to evaluate your personal strengths and weaknesses, which allows you to grow as a person. This can be of great benefit to you as it sends you on a journey of self-discovery. You learn to be more compassionate and can grow from your negative attributes. As a result, you develop a strong sense of who you are.

When it comes to anxiety, if you are able to use the tools adopted in self-acceptance, you will be able to begin evaluating your own anxiety and pinpoint your issues. When you can do this, it becomes easier to identify and resolve the things that cause your anxiety.

What is Self-Acceptance and Why is it Important?

Self-acceptance is a process of evaluating your own personal strengths and weaknesses, and this knowledge helps you grow as a person. It provides you with the ability to accept any negative attributes you feel you have and develop them. It gives you a strong sense of self.

There are many benefits of tapping into self-acceptance, as this allows you to get comfortable with who you are and opens up the doors to practicing self-love. It can also help you improve your self-esteem, develop your self-control, and strengthen interpersonal relationships you have with others. In addition to this, it can help to improve your anxiety symptoms.

By exploring self-acceptance techniques, you'll be able to have more control over your negative thinking patterns and will be able to work towards stopping them completely.

So many people heighten their levels of anxiety because of negative self-talk or thinking. How many times have you told yourself...

> *"There's something wrong with me."*

> *"I'm just not good enough."*

"I'll never be able to do that."

This negativity gets you down and lowers your self-esteem, but while you believe the issue is you not doing something well enough, it's more likely to be a simple mindset issue, rather than anything else.

The aim of self-acceptance is to help you come to terms with being you. If you do have anxiety, you can accept this is a struggle for you, and it's real, and once you know this, you know you can fight against it. This is a good thing, as it's good to embrace acceptance. If you can master self-acceptance, there's no doubt that you can also overcome your anxiety symptoms in a way that allows you to still live your life to the fullest.

It's time you see yourself as someone who is capable of overcoming the barriers that anxiety places in front of you, so you can live your best life. We want you to love and appreciate yourself, and stay optimistic when facing anxious thoughts and gain the confidence to question their viability.

But how can you become self-acceptant?

5 Steps to Self-Acceptance

Sometimes, it's not easy to recognize our positive attributes. In fact, many people struggle to see the good in themselves, and, therefore, they can't accept themselves. While this is common, there are five steps you can take to self-acceptance:

1. Admit and Acknowledge

To start the process, you need to own up to how you feel and acknowledge that feeling; it's okay to feel how you feel. If you feel upset, embarrassed, or angry, you may not like yourself right now. Maybe you feel something is wrong with you or you are not good enough. Whatever you are feeling, it's important to recognize it and acknowledge that this is how you feel. You'll be surprised at how powerful this first step is. Write down how you feel at first as this will help you to go through the 5-step process effectively.

2. Time to Challenge

This next step is quite tricky, especially if you've been experiencing negative thought patterns for some time. The key is to try and recognize the negative thoughts as soon as they make their appearance. Writing them down can prompt you when you have the same thought again in the future. Once you've identified some of your negative thoughts, try to acknowledge them and let them go. If you feel 'you can't do something,' think of a reason why you can, then take a deep breath, remind yourself of the positive reason that you can do it, then blow away your negative thought as you exhale. Just let them float away.

3. Be Kind

We are naturally hard on ourselves, but it's important to be kind and gentle to ourselves when needed. We all make mistakes, and sometimes, we need time and space to heal. If we are overly critical of ourselves, it leads to more unhappiness and causes self-loathing. Take an approach that allows you to be your own best friend by talking in a respectful way to yourself, give yourself compliments and do things that make you happy.

4. Goal Setting

Accept Who You Are

A good way to focus on accepting yourself is to set goals. Your goals can be about anything you want, so start thinking about what you want in life from fitness to careers and personal development. Break your goals down by creating smaller steps on how you can achieve them. For example, if your goal is to pass an exam, you may make a list of all the topics you need to cover in order to have the best chance. You may then want to study each area (ticking off the topics as you go), speak to your teacher to see how you can improve it, complete a practice exam, revise for the real exam, use calming techniques before the exam, and then sit the exam. All of these steps help you achieve an overall goal, and ticking them off as you go helps you stay motivated. This works if your goals are also related to self-improvement.

5. Be with Positive People

It's a good idea to be with other positive people, in fact, you should surround yourself with them. Negative people bring you down, so you should be with people who make you feel good, care about you, and want to help and encourage you. Being with others who are positive can motivate you and they can provide information and advice to you, and they may even notice qualities that you don't even know you have. Our family and friends see the good in us, and this makes us feel good about ourselves.

Learning self-acceptance is a journey in itself, and it's a process. If you begin practicing the steps now, it will start to impact your anxiety in more ways than you know. This won't happen instantly but knowing these steps will set you off on the right track to self-acceptance.

Self-Acceptance Activities

Learning self-acceptance is one of the best things you can do for yourself, as it improves your general mental health, but in the beginning, it takes you out of your comfort zone. Give yourself time and be forgiving because it won't happen overnight. The shift takes time.

The best thing to do is follow the steps to self-acceptance in the section above. There are also some activities you can do to kick-start this process, by getting to know the real you:

1. List your strengths – what are you good at? What do your friends or family come to you about? What are you passionate about? Learning about the things we are good at gives us a real boost. You can even ask your friends and family what they think your strengths are. You may be surprised!
2. Ask others what they like about you – this can really help you recognize your personal qualities. You will soon see how important and unique you are.
3. Write lists about the things you like:
    a. What are your favorite gifts?
    b. What are your hobbies?
    c. What are your aspirations in life?
    d. How do you envision your ideal life (think career, personal life, living arrangements, material things, how you would feel if you had this life)?
    e. Favorite foods and drinks
    f. Top ten places you'd like to visit

g. Movies and songs you like

h. What makes you happy?

You're probably wondering what the purpose of this is, but knowing these things helps you discover who you are. When you know yourself inside and out, and know how others value you, you can start to see your purpose. When you have a purpose, you have the motivation to overcome your anxious symptoms and any other barriers that effect you being who you want to be or doing what you want to do.

Remember, mild anxiety is a part of life, but by knowing yourself and embracing self-acceptance, you can begin to conquer the things that cause or trigger your anxiety to an uncontrollable level.

Now you know how to work on self-acceptance, we can start to tackle the triggers.

Chapter 4

Know Your Triggers

Have you ever witnessed something that's caused a reaction? This could be on television, in person, or even just something you've read or heard. It causes you to feel angry, upset, or sometimes even happy. This is a trigger.

When you have anxious symptoms and they spiral, there's usually a root cause. Something causes those feelings you're experiencing; if you really want to get your anxiety under control, knowing your triggers is extremely important. In this chapter, we'll talk more in-depth about your triggers so you can evaluate your anxiety. We'll talk about why it's important to know your triggers, while also exploring how knowing your triggers can help you prevent or avoid anxiety, if possible.

Let's focus on triggers, so you can start to work out yours.

9 Common Anxiety Triggers

When we talk about anxiety triggers, they are the things that stimulate anxiety symptoms and push them to the surface. There are many things that can trigger anxiety and we're going to talk through some of those.

1. Social anxiety – you'll have probably heard the term social anxiety, but just to clarify, this is when you feel anxious about being in a social setting. Let's say you're going to a concert or a big family event, but your heart quickens, you have sweaty palms, and you even feel sick at the thought of going. If the thought of going to a social event triggers your anxiety and you don't deal with it, this could escalate and cause you to avoid such gatherings.

2. Sleep deprivation – anxiety is closely linked with sleep. Sleep disturbances and disorders can be a sign of anxiety or stress. If you can't sleep because you're anxious, then you're tired during the day because you didn't sleep well enough. It's important to build a good sleep routine to prevent this.

3. Medications – sometimes, medication can trigger anxiety. It tends to be the medication that impacts your brain chemistry, which can include things like stimulants, decongestants, and steroids. You should speak to your doctor if you suspect that medication is triggering your anxiety, as they'll be able to provide you with some advice.

4. Caffeine – caffeine is a stimulant, and therefore it can increase anxiety. It can impact your sleep, and it can also alter your mood. If you drink a lot of caffeine and believe it could be a trigger for your anxiety, you should consider cutting down or weaning yourself off it completely. Giving up caffeine isn't always so easy, so it can take time!

5. Money worries – if you or your family have money worries, it can trigger your anxiety. If we don't have enough money, it can prevent us from doing the things

we want to do. It can also prevent us from getting the necessities, which can cause extreme worry, which causes anxiety. Learning more about managing finances or getting some help with finances can really help. Don't be afraid to seek help before things get out of control.

6. Stress – if you're stressed, this can lead to anxiety. Many people feel stressed due to job or education pressures, but sometimes there are issues within the family that cause you stress too. If you feel stressed out, you need to try and figure out why, i.e., to understand the root cause. You can also use calming techniques such as breathing exercises or meditation to calm the mind initially, so you can start to think about things in a logical way.

7. Life events – when things happen in our lives that cause change, it can trigger our anxiety. When a person switches careers, or if divorce happens to you or within your family, anxiety can flair up. It takes time for everyone to adjust, so plan small steps in advance when you know changes are coming. That way, you're in control.

8. Negative Self-Talk – being hard on yourself can trigger anxiety. If you start listening to your negative self-talk, it can be difficult for you to battle through and interrupt those patterns. It's important that you learn how to deal with mistakes or the difficult situations you find yourself in, effectively. Cognitive Behavioral Therapy can help you get to grips with your negative self-talk.

9. Conflict – if you've ever fallen out with someone or had a conflict with another person, you may have

experienced anxiety. Conflict often triggers anxious thoughts, because we can feel frustrated if we can't remedy a situation, or if we don't know how to deal with it. It can cause a lot of internal upset, but often, learning conflict resolution techniques or talking to a therapist can help you manage conflict better.

Do any of the 9 most common causes of anxiety resonate with you?

Of course, there may be other situations that cause anxiety that doesn't fit perfectly into any of these categories, but recognizing your triggers is the first step to dealing with your anxiety. It's important for you to understand why knowing this is so important, so let's find out...

Why is it Important to Know My Triggers?

As you know, there are many things that could trigger your anxiety but if you know what sets you off, you can prevent them from happening in the future, or you can minimize their risk and manage the impact this has on you.

There's nothing simple about anxiety. It's a complex issue, but it affects millions of people all over the world. The symptoms and triggers are different for everyone, so people who are anxious have their own unique experiences, hence, managing anxiety can be complicated. You use different tools and techniques to manage your symptoms and triggers, but then, it's up to you to implement them. Nobody can take them away or resolve them for you.

When you learn to identify what's triggering your anxiety symptoms, you can figure out how to stop your anxiety from becoming extremely overwhelming and out of control. While anxiety is sometimes a normal response, it can encourage us to become irrational. It might not take the anxiety away, but it can lessen its severity, and the severity of the other symptoms you're suffering from as part of your anxiety.

The last thing you want is for your anxiety to get worse!

How Can Knowing My Triggers Help Me Avoid or Prevent Anxiety Symptoms?

Close your eyes and think about a time you felt anxiety...

- *Where were you?*
- *What were you doing?*
- *What symptoms of anxiety did you present?*
- *How did it make you feel?*
- *Why do you think it happened (think back to the moment the feelings of anxiety heightened, and what may have caused this episode)?*
- *Is there anything in the environment you're in that could have caused this?*
- *Is your anxiety connected to a person?*
- *Is there anything you did or didn't say, or should or shouldn't have done?*
- *In an ideal world, what would've happened? How could you have dealt with this differently?*

Anxiety triggers are often associated to the negative emotions we experience when something goes wrong. Sometimes the triggers are less serious, for example, it could be because you've not had enough sleep, you've had an argument with someone, or due to your procrastinating. Knowing your anxiety triggers helps you avoid or prevent anxiety because you ultimately make a choice to deal with them.

To identify your anxiety triggers, you should:

- Listen to your body – our body sends us warning signals when we're stressed or anxious, so check in with yourself. If you're feeling anxious, take some time to relax and reflect. What happened leading up to this? What is your behavior like? Are there any triggers that spring to mind (poor diet, too much caffeine, insomnia)? You can then remedy the issue; if you're tired, try to sleep or rest to remedy your anxiety.

- Be honest – it isn't always easy to come to terms with our anxiety and it can be difficult to figure out its origin. If it manifests, it could become out of control. Be honest with yourself and talk about how you feel, as it will help you find the peace you need when tackling your anxiety.

- Journaling – if you write a journal that details your thoughts and feelings, you can start keeping track of when your anxiety occurs, and you could spot patterns. You should journal both the positive and negative times because knowing what makes you feel great can help you to figure out how to stop an attack from escalating.

- Therapy – sometimes anxiety is connected to mental health issues or trauma, and this means you could benefit from a therapist who can help you deep dive, find the root cause, and motivate you to deal with these issues. They can provide you with techniques to help you deal with your anxiety and relieve your symptoms.

When it comes to anxiety, you're not alone. Only when you've identified your triggers can you start to approach each cause, and learn to overcome it. When you're exploring your anxiety symptoms, it's a good opportunity to get to know yourself a little more. This is your path to overcoming your anxiety, so you must shape it.

While this chapter talks about identifying and analyzing your triggers, the next chapter will take you a step further as you'll begin to explore how to find out more when it comes to your anxiety. We'll talk about research, and how this can help you to overcome your feelings of anxiety. Once you've considered this, it's time to forge a plan of action.

Let's kick those symptoms to the curb!

Chapter 5

Research the Enemy

"The enemy of my enemy is my friend."

~ Ancient Proverb (Unknown)

When you know what's triggering your anxiety and causing your symptoms, you need to deep-dive and explore your reasons behind this. Researching the reason for your anxiety is extremely important but figuring out why you feel anxious takes time.

In this chapter, we're going to explore how getting to the root cause can really help you remedy any of the symptoms you suffer and how to take the next step in understanding your anxiety and the true meaning behind it.

Some anxiety is inevitable, so researching the triggers can help you assess whether your anxiety is a normal reaction or something that requires your attention.

Let's talk about the type of research you SHOULD do...

What Kind of Research Should I Do When it Comes to My Anxiety?

While we touched on some of the symptoms of anxiety already, it's time to commit to exploring your triggers. This is the thing that causes you to suffer from your symptoms of anxiety.

Let's look at an example...

Sally must deliver a presentation in front of a group of people today. Her palms are sweaty, her heart is racing, and she's experiencing a lot of negative self-talk. She's questioning whether she can go through with it.

Now, it's having to deliver the presentation in front of a group of people that is likely causing her anxiety, but she needs to get to the bottom of what's really causing it. Most people are anxious or nervous when they have to speak in front of a group, so this is a normal reaction. Her symptoms such as sweating, can't be helped, as they are a normal symptom of anxiety, as is a racing heart. Such symptoms alone would not indicate that Sally has anxiety, but it can be a sign that she is anxious or nervous. The aim of this book is to raise awareness of all anxiety symptoms, but simply having sweaty palms or a racing heart would not mean that the person would be diagnosed with anxiety. If a person has to speak in public, both of these things can be a normal reaction to the situation, but they will usually subside quite quickly. If they happen regularly, along with other symptoms, then it may be a sign that anxiety is spiraling.

The negative self-talk is likely to express vital information about the type of anxiety she's feeling. For instance, she could be telling herself:

- *You're going to make a mistake.*
- *People are going to laugh at you.*
- *The audience probably won't be able to hear you.*
- *You're going to be put on the spot with questions you can't answer.*
- *People don't want to listen to what you want to say.*
- *You don't know enough about the topic.*
- *Your technology is likely to fail.*
- *You're going to sound stupid.*
- *You're not good at speaking to groups.*

The list could go on but imagine having to listen to this (or similar) negative self-talk, over and over.

The point that we need to figure out is why we feel like this.

While sweating more, or racing hearts are normal, such symptoms can simply indicate a slight nervousness before the speech which is not out of the ordinary. Often, this will pass once they're on stage, but if it is more intense, it can sometimes be remedied by learning to calm your mind through breathing exercises or meditation, for example, the negative self-talk is a little more complex. This could be down to a lack of confidence. Lack of confidence is a common anxiety trigger.

Sally then needs to research her confidence issues when it comes to public speaking, because this is the root of the matter. To do this, she has to consider a series of questions:

- She should think back to her earliest memory of lacking confidence and consider the events surrounding this. *What happened to trigger this? What happened before, during, and after?*
- Has she ever spoken publicly before, and if so, what happened?
- Does she lack confidence in other areas, and if so, what?

What should Sally do?

She should research the solutions to her triggers, which include:

- Ways to build her self-confidence
- How to eradicate negative self-talk
- Strategies to develop her presentation and speaking skills
- Breathing exercises or meditation techniques to calm the mind

Working on a solution means she's taking positive action toward dealing with her anxiety. She should also keep a journal of the times she experiences anxiety and highlight if confidence appears to be the cause. She can then learn to identify occurrences, and causes, and start to do something about this.

Researching how to combat the cause or trigger of your anxiety is critical to overcoming it, and it can increase your understanding of your anxious tendencies. The more you understand, the more you can overcome.

Why is it Important to Understand What Makes Me Feel Anxious?

Anxiety escalates because we ignore it at first. We don't like it. It's our worse enemy. We don't like how it makes us feel or act, and we certainly don't like the way it limits our beliefs. Dealing with anxiety is a challenge, but in order to succeed at this challenge, you need to be able to understand your anxiety.

Anxiety presents itself differently for everyone and as mentioned in the earlier section, it's never one single symptom, it's a multitude of symptoms and feelings that build and build. Many people suffer intense emotions like a whirlwind swirling around them, but for others, it builds momentum over time. If you understand what makes you feel anxious, you can start to put together your own toolbox of strategies and comforts that help you to deal with it effectively, by addressing each symptom.

Remember, not every symptom of anxiety needs to be treated as a certain level of anxiety is normal, and it can even be healthy. Often, if we're nervous or anxious about a job interview, it shows we care, and therefore our anxiety can spur us into action—we show our best self. If our palms are sweaty or our heart races, it's normal! Anxiety also acts as a warning sign of danger. If you're walking down a dark street late at night, your anxiety is the thing that encourages you to be more aware of your surroundings and alert to possible dangers. If you feel something is about to happen, it spurs you into a survival-like action to protect yourself. This could be something as simple as running to a lit area or shouting for help. We don't need to treat these symptoms, because anxiety isn't a problem at this point.

Knowing what makes you suffer from your anxious symptoms helps you to:

- Develop bodily awareness – anxiety doesn't just impact your mind; it also affects the body. If you recognize your bodily symptoms of anxiety like sweating, shallow breathing, or even a stomach- or headache, you can use this opportunity to challenge your anxiety before it gets worse.
- Intervene to prevent or stop the anxiety attack from escalating – anxiety often snowballs, so once you get it, it starts to build. The best thing to do is prevent it or stop it. This takes practice, as you need to identify your triggers first and then calm your mind.
- Live a normal life, while managing your anxiety – anxiety stops you from living your life when it's out of control. It limits you! But if you learn the strategies that help to keep it under control, it can mean you don't have to live within the limitations that anxiety is placing on your life. You can beat it!
- Examine your day-to-day activities – anxiety helps you to consider the activities you take part in every day, as they may be causing you anxiety without you even realizing it. Sometimes, we believe our anxiety stems from a traumatic or big event in our life, but the small things that we don't even think about can be contributing too. Paying attention and showing awareness for all activities ensure that anxiety isn't able to shape your life.
- See the benefit of experiencing anxiety – sometimes a little bit of anxiety gives us a warning or makes us feel excited about life. It can motivate and help you feel accomplished because if you feel anxious and still

'do' the things you want to do, you're overcoming your anxiety, so you've succeeded. Eventually, you'll be able to tell the difference between the type of anxiety that is problematic, in comparison to the healthy sort.

Researching your anxiety and its triggers is extremely important for your recovery.

Let's talk about how it can help.

How Can Researching My Anxiety Help Me Overcome it?

Once you research your anxiety symptoms and their triggers, it helps you make a plan of action, so you can deal with it. We've talked about some of the ways to overcome your anxiety already, but if you research what's really causing your triggers, you can start to work on challenging them.

It will also help you realize what must be done to prevent that trigger from becoming a problem in the long-term. Now, some anxiety symptoms are inevitable. For example, perhaps someone feels anxious when home alone. If they live alone, this may be something they can't completely resist, but that doesn't mean they can't research the trigger to help understand why they feel that way so that they can do something about it. If the concern is to do with home invasion for instance, they could put security measures in place to make their home safer, while also having a plan of action to practice being alone and making the most of it.

Your research should include monitoring yourself and to see if there are any noticeable patterns when it comes to your anxious symptoms, through journalling, but you should also research further (this could be online if you wish), so you can educate yourself and overcome the issue.

We mentioned confidence being an issue earlier in this chapter, so if you research different ways to build your confidence and schedule time in for this, you can make it a priority to develop this.

Sometimes, when we're super-anxious, we don't really understand why we're feeling that way, and to be honest, we don't really think about it. Learning to be more self-aware and researching your anxiety issues, symptoms, and triggers can help you to cope with the feelings of anxiety you're experiencing.

Once you've researched the triggers and know where they stem from, you need to create your goals. With each symptom, trigger, and root cause, you should set yourself a goal.

Simply close your eyes and visualize how you would deal with your symptom, trigger or root cause, in an ideal world. This will help you create your goals!

Your goals will help you to form your plan of attack... which we'll discuss in the next chapter. The whole of Section 2 focuses on reducing your anxiety, permanently.

Section 2: Managing Your Anxiety

Chapter 6

Plan of Attack

"Anxiety's like a rocking chair. It gives you something to do, but it doesn't get you very far."

~ Jodi Picoult

In this section, we're going to work through strategies that will help you manage your anxiety. It's time to force your plan of attack against your symptoms of anxiety. If you're:

- Tired of being controlled by your anxiety symptoms
- Ready to work on managing your anxiety levels
- Determined to get on with your life happily
- Already aware of what's triggering or causing your anxiety symptoms
- Motivated – you want to address your anxiety and its triggers

You're in the right place. Because you're ready to create your plan of attack. In this chapter, we're going to talk about the next step, once you've accepted yourself, identified your triggers, and researched your anxiety.

We're also going to talk through the importance of planning, and how you can develop the right plan of action.

What Should I Do After Accepting Myself, Identifying My Triggers, and Researching the Anxiety?

You've taken huge steps throughout this section already. You've taken action to accept yourself, you know how to identify your triggers, and you also know the importance of researching your anxiety to get to its root cause.

You've made excellent progress if you are beginning to apply the skills we've learned to find out all about your anxiety, so now, it's time to form your plan of attack.

That's right, it's time to head into battle!

The first thing you should do is establish a daily routine. Consider the tasks you complete on a daily basis and include the times you wake up, eat meals, go to bed, work, and exercise.

Write a list of the things you do every day (or almost every day).

Write further lists detailing the tasks you do less regularly, i.e., weekly or monthly.

Your lists will help you form your routine!

You may also want to consider hydrating yourself and exercising first thing in the morning, planning in healthy meals and snacks each day, and stopping your screentime at least an hour before bed (fill this time with a relaxing bath, reading a book, or writing in your journal). Once you've established your basic routine, you can start to plan actionable steps to help you combat your symptoms of anxiety.

Your anxiety action plan doesn't have to be complicated. You've started doing the work already, so you can create your action plan in three easy steps.

1. Be constantly aware – recognize your feelings of anxiety and acknowledge them by calling them by their name. Don't hide them.
2. Challenge them – sometimes we feel anxious, but the root cause is not even true. For example, if you're telling yourself you're not good enough, ask yourself, *Where's the evidence?* Sometimes we live a false narrative, so always question your thoughts, challenge your anxieties, and call them out; *are they the truths?*
3. Share – if you try to deal with anxiety alone, you're in danger of closing yourself off from the world. We heal best if we can speak about the things that concern us, if we have a safe place, and if we have strong relationships with others.

Your plan needs to allow you time to heal, and you can only heal if you follow the steps above. It could involve taking small steps, such as building up awareness first. You can build strategies into your schedule to ensure you're battling against your anxiety.

For example, if you want to work on developing your awareness of your anxiety, you could decide to keep a journal or log to detail your anxiety episodes. This means you can note down your symptoms, what caused it, and what happened as a result. You can then set time in your schedule daily to go through those details and analyze the information. This allows you to challenge your actions.

*Write down how you'll respond next time: *What do you wish you'd done instead? What is the root of the matter? What can you do next time? Is there anything that will remedy those symptoms?*

Once you've built up your awareness, you need to think about your healing time. You need to do some experimentation here and find out what eases your anxiety. There are some common activities that ease general anxiety, so you could:

- Use breathing techniques. There are simple breathing techniques that can calm you down.
  - Breathe in slowly, gently, but deeply for 5 seconds
  - Hold your breath for 3 seconds
  - Slowly breathe out. Exhale the whole breath for around 7 seconds
  - Repeat approximately 10 times or until you begin to feel calm. Focus on your breathing until you are calm.
- Exercise. This can certainly help you beat your symptoms of anxiety as it helps to burn your stresses away, encourages you to breathe in a healthier way, provides you with a distraction, and it releases endorphins into your brain that help to control your mood. Many people with anxiety who build exercise into their schedule notice a reduction in their anxiety. Exercise should be at a level you can manage, so a simple walk, hitting the gym, or taking a class can all help.

Plan of Attack

- Talk about it. If you're feeling anxious, it's best to talk about it to someone you like and trust. Anxiety has a bad habit of making us feel alone, but to beat it, you really need to talk about it. Just let them know how you feel, and if they're good people, they'll listen, support you, and maybe even boost your mood.
- Relax. When we're anxious, we're the opposite of relaxed. In order to beat anxiety, we need to relax and calm our minds. Figure out what relaxes you and build this into your plan. This means, when your anxiety increases, you can soothe your symptoms by relaxing. This could be something simple as taking a walk on the beach or in the woods, taking a warm bath, or meditating.
- Learn how to manage your negative self-talk. A lot of anxiety comes from your negative self-talk, as the negative thoughts spiral. You put yourself down, increasing your anxiety. It's not always easy to stop it from happening, but you can challenge it by doing the following:
    - Create a checklist of questions that you can answer when you experience negative self-talk.
        - What evidence is there to confirm that negative self-talk is true?
        - Is there a reason to believe something is wrong?
        - Could I be blowing this out of proportion?
    - Create affirmations that you can regularly repeat to yourself, to make you feel better. Things like:
        - I can do 'something/it.'

- I am grateful for my life and feel extremely lucky.
- I am beating my anxiety; it doesn't control me.
- When I face limitations caused by my anxiety, I overcome them.
- I'm excited for tomorrow as I have a great life.

Schedule some activities into your daily routine that ease your anxiety symptoms, as they may help you keep your anxiety under control. Remember, your plan of attack should work for you, and you should take this at your own pace. Some people need to take small steps, while others are ready to dive right in. Regardless of your pace, make sure you have a strategy for handling each symptom and working on each cause and trigger. For example, if your heart starts racing, you could use your breathing techniques to calm down.

Battling your anxiety symptoms can be uncomfortable at times, even for the most successful people, confronting their fears is not an easy task. However, the sense of accomplishment you'll feel when you face your fears and begin to beat your anxiety will boost your confidence going forward. It gets easier over time!

Overcoming your anxiety symptoms is a journey, so if you can learn to accept you have talents and strengths, identify triggers of your anxiety, and research the causes of your anxiety, you will already know how you want to start confronting those fears. Ultimately, it's down to you to fight against anxiety so you can make progress and overcome your fears.

Plan of Attack

*Write down 2-3 causes of your anxiety and quickly outline the action you could take to beat them.

*If you suffer one of your symptoms unexpectedly, you'll know exactly what to do. In time, it will hardly affect your life at all.

Why is it Important to Plan Accordingly?

Research shows that keeping a steady routine improves your mental health and can help to keep your anxiety at bay. It's important that you create a suitable plan of attack when it comes to your anxiety, and this includes creating day-to-day routines and specific steps that help you combat your specific anxiety symptoms. Your plan must help you progress, for example, if your anxiety was because you hate being home alone, the answer is not to simply lock yourself inside for a week in hopes you have time to overcome the fear. Your plan should be much more strategic.

Too much too soon could set you into a wave of panic, so the best thing to do is practice being alone in short steps. When you start to feel anxious because you're alone, plan some strategies to help deal with those symptoms. Some people are simply lonely, and therefore don't like being alone, so if this is the case, staying alone for a few hours at a time and distracting yourself with a hobby or activity can prevent you from the negative thinking patterns that are sparking your symptoms.

Another example includes public speaking. If this is something you're anxious about, practice doing this in small steps. Set yourself goals, so next time you're in a team meeting, you ask a question. Do the same next time you're on a training course or conference. After this, you should speak about a topic for around 5 minutes, practice speaking in front of family and friends, and then build your speaking confidence over time. By starting on a smaller scale and slowly moving into a larger crowd, you can slowly overcome your fear.

If you make the right plan of action and plan accordingly, in line with your triggers and symptoms, you won't simply fix your anxiety in the short term, it will become a long-term solution. It's likely that your anxiety will not wholly disappear. Remember, some anxiety is good for you anyway, but it will be at a manageable level, so you can still live the life you want to live, without worrying about the limitations.

How Can Planning the Right Action Help Me Overcome Anxiety?

If you have the right strategy in place to beat your anxiety, it can help you feel more comfortable as you address your concerns. You will also know what to do, so you won't be left in limbo, which means you're not leaving things to chance, but you must make sure that the plan of action you have is the right plan.

Doing the background work so you understand your anxiety and its triggers in greater depth is extremely important because your plan of action will only work if you're addressing your anxiety effectively. You can only plan to overcome the anxiety causes and triggers if you know what they are. If your anxiety is having to speak in front of a large group of people, it would not be effective to plan actionable steps that help you overcome a fear of exam stress. Your plan must help you address your anxiety triggers in relation to speaking in front of large groups.

Plan of Attack

If you plan to overcome your symptoms of anxiety in the right way, you will get back control of your life. It's the view of many people that if we have anxiety, we should ignore it, but this is very wrong. Ignoring anxiety can lead to further health problems, so you must take this seriously. If you get the right treatment, which sometimes means seeing a therapist, you will beat your anxiety and overcome the limitations it presents for you.

People who develop anxiety disorders and don't develop the right plan of action often find that they struggle with employment opportunities, lose education, and have difficulties maintaining relationships with family, friends, and partners.

A positive routine, and a plan of action that includes relevant anxiety beating strategies are crucial to beating your anxiety. Then all you need to do is prevent it!

Chapter 7

Mind, Body, and Spirit

While we've looked at evaluating anxiety a lot in the previous chapters, it's time to delve deeper into treating your anxiety symptoms. When you're working on combatting anxiety, you need to work on several aspects of your life. You have a great plan already, but now it's time to reduce your anxiety altogether.

We've discussed some ways of battling anxiety already, but in order to find a long-term solution, let's talk about your well-being, which includes your mind, body, and spirit.

What is the First Thing to Manage When Trying to Prevent Anxiety?

If you want to manage and prevent anxiety, it's important to consider your lifestyle as a whole. Anyone who has any kind of mental health issues or worries should focus on eating healthily, exercising, and getting enough sleep because it's proven those things can help reduce the symptoms associated with anxiousness.

Living a healthy lifestyle is always a good place to start. You have formed your initial plan of action to confront your anxiety, so keeping up with your daily schedule can really help. Ensuring that you:

- Drink plenty of water to stay hydrated, especially when you first wake up
- Ensure you're eating healthy meals and snacks
- Exercise daily for at least 20-30 minutes
- Make sure you're getting enough sleep and schedule in time to wind down. It's recommended that you get between 7.5-9 hours of sleep every night

In addition to this, when you consider your well-being and lifestyle as a whole, you must consider how you care for your mind, body, and spirit.

Let's discuss your mind first of all as this is often where your anxiety begins. It becomes filled with thoughts, fears, and worries that you just can't shift. We've already discussed how a busy, anxious mind needs to be calmed and there are a number of ways you can do this:

- Meditating and breathing exercises can't be recommended enough. This can really provide you with focus and help you calm your mind by focusing on your breathing and then other positive outcomes, aspirations, and visuals.
- CBT (cognitive behavioral therapy) can also help you put things into perspective.
- Taking a walk in a place you love can distract your mind.
- Speaking affirmations regularly throughout the day to calm your mind and encourage positive thinking can help to combat your negative self-talk.

- Reading a book is a great way for your mind to escape.
- Writing a diary or journal can distract your mind and shift your focus.
- Talking therapies with a therapist or anxiety support group. Talking can really help you determine how to put things into perspective.
- Practice staying in the present. If your mind is going over something from the past, over and over, simply consider the circumstances and ask yourself if your coping abilities or knowledge have changed since this event. Accept that it happened and refocus on the now.
- Challenge your thoughts with questions. If you're having negative thoughts regularly, it's time to start questioning them. Consider if the thought is true. Is it helpful? Not all true thoughts are helpful, and if a thought is demotivating you, it's not going to help. Focus your attention on something that is helpful and move on. Just let it go!
- Play your 'feeling happy and motivated' song playlist. Singing raises your vibration and can certainly increase your level of happiness. If you haven't already, create a playlist of those songs that make you feel happy and keep you feeling motivated. Add this to your schedule—for example, listen to them when you go out for your morning walk or run.

It's also important to take care of your body. There are many ways to do this, including:

- Exercising daily. Make sure you do some 15-20 minutes cardio to look after heart, and 5-10 minutes of strengthening and stretching if possible as this will help to condition your body.

- Get a massage. A massage can help your body relax and relieve any tension you feel. Tension and stress is often a sign of anxiety, but once we are calm in mind and body, we can think about things more logically.
- Eat nutritious food. Eating healthily can prevent anxiety and its impact on the body. As a general rule, make sure you're eating plenty of fruit or vegetables, while also ensuring you take your recommended daily allowance (RDA) of carbohydrates, proteins, healthy fats, and dairy. The RDA depends on numerous factors, such as your age and gender. The best vitamins and minerals for anxiety and stress include:
  - Vitamins B, C, D, and A
  - Omega 3
  - Selenium
  - Magnesium

So, you should ensure your diet is rich in those things.

- Take a bath. Soaking your muscles in a warm bath can help you melt away your stresses and anxieties. It's a great way to calm the mind, while also taking care of your body.
- Book a treatment at the salon or spa, such as a facial, a haircut, a manicure or pedicure, a body wrap, or use the saunas or pools.

Now, that's your body and mind well cared for, *but what about your spirit?* Spiritually, your anxiety is stealing the ability for you to enjoy life, which means you're living with negative thoughts or feelings of hopelessness. It's basically your mental energy and you can change this!

Mind, Body, and Spirit

Being spiritual changes your whole energy from negative to positive. If your spirit is out of alignment, it's letting you know that something isn't quite right, or you need to fix something. Finding inner balance can help with how you feel, spiritually. You should make sure you're still using your breathing techniques, socializing, resting or meditating, and taking some quiet time just for you. It's all about you being in touch with the inner you, and aligning what you do to what you want in life.

If you are:

1. Able to identify your core values and purpose in life
2. Working on achieving your full potential

You can certainly become more spiritual and use any anxiety you feel to your advantage. There are other ways to become more spiritual, while also working on your mind and body at the same time...

- Yoga
- Tai-Chi
- Qigong

Each of these practices involve a form of exercise, but the exercises help to both exercise AND care for the body, while such practices also involve deep breathing and calming your mind. It's believed that more than half of people with anxiety who regularly take part in yoga have found that their levels of anxiety decrease within a few short weeks.

When you incorporate strategies to take care of your mind, body, and spirit into your schedule, this has to be a long-term commitment. Many people believe they don't have time to schedule such strategies to ensure they take care of their well-being, however, consider this question...

Do you have time to keep being held back, over and over again, because of your anxiety?

It's a no-brainer really!

Taking care of your well-being is an extremely important part of your long-term plan to beat your symptoms. Let's explain why.

Why is it Important to Consider My Well-being?

You are important. Anxiety symptoms often show their ugly head or they get worse because we aren't taking care of ourselves. If you want to get the best out of yourself, you have to balance this out by taking care of your own well-being.

Studies show that those who take care of their own well-being develop practical coping skills that stay with them for the rest of their life, and are able to thrive, regardless of their anxiety struggles. They also notice:

- A reduction in the anxiety they feel
- Mood improves
- They can think more clearly
- A greater sense of inner peace and calm
- Relationships improve
- Their self-esteem increases
- A decrease in depression
- Their memory sharpens

- They develop better sleeping patterns
- Resilience increases
- Their problem-solving skills improve

The list simply names a few, as the benefits of taking care of yourself do not stop here. We often experience anxiety in three ways:

1. Neurotic anxiety, which is basically the unconscious worry you feel that causes you to overthink every situation. This can be difficult to control, so it's important to keep on top of this.
2. Reality anxiety, which refers to anxiety you feel based on real, negative situations in your life such as fear of illness, and other physical events such as fearing a threatening object (or people) when you're close to them.
3. Moral anxiety, which means you fear going against your own principles. This usually occurs because you want to do something different to what you normally do.

All three types of anxiety have an impact on your mind, body, and spirit, but if you take care of yourself, symptoms are less likely to be as aggressive. If you don't take care of your well-being, you're at risk of suffering both mentally and physically because of your anxiety, but if you do take action, you can live the life you want.

How Can I Begin to Incorporate a Healthier Lifestyle?

It's not difficult to adopt a healthier lifestyle. It's all about taking it slow and making small changes that, over time, make a big difference. We have already talked about eating healthier, taking vitamin supplements, exercising, and meditating, but if you need things to start off at a slower pace, we have put together some awesome tips to help you.

When you're trying to achieve something in life, it's best to have a goal. So, before you go any further, think about your goal when it comes to anxiety. *In an ideal world, what would your goal be? How would your life be different without anxiety?*

Now you've got that, ask yourself *why? Why do you want your life to be free from anxiety's control? How would your life be different?*

Your goal and purpose provide you with direction and motivation when it comes to beating your anxiety symptoms. For instance, some people want to keep their anxiety at a controllable level, to improve their relationships with their family. Focusing on a positive outcome can drive us toward achieving this goal.

When it comes to the mind, you should:

- Have some quiet time: you don't have to do anything. Make yourself a refreshment and sit quietly. You can reflect on your day if you wish.
- If you're struggling with meditation, this is normal. Meditation isn't always an easy thing to embrace. It can be difficult, and it takes time to work. As you don't

necessarily see the benefit instantaneously, and, it focuses a lot on your mindset, many people quit before they've really started. If you're struggling with meditation, you should:

- Start small – 5-10 minutes at a time
- Ensure you're in a quiet place, without distraction
- Try a short, guided meditation (there are many available for free or paid through apps, and even on platforms such as YouTube)
- Commit to meditation every day, for at least a month

- Use a calming fragrance, such as lavender. It's known for its calming properties. A simple scent such as lavender can really help to bring back mental calm.
- Take a social media break. Sometimes social media is the root of our anxieties. Taking a break can help you get back to reality and free yourself from the mental clutter and negativity that social media sometimes brings.
- Avoid caffeine. Caffeine is a stimulant, so if you find that your mind is constantly active and struggles to calm down, you should certainly reduce or avoid it

Calming the mind can often help with the physical symptoms of anxiety too, for example, meditating and relaxing can help if your heart is racing. If your body is suffering due to symptoms of anxiety, you could:

- Try stretching, rather than completing a more active exercise regime. If you're not used to high-intensity exercise, start slow, by completing some stretches.

They can help to relieve tension and they can even alleviate symptoms of pain.

When it comes to spirituality, many people don't know where to start. You should:

- Ensure you're clear of your purpose, so you know why you're constantly working on beating your anxiety.
- Ensure you are embracing healthier habits. Keeping your habits in check is better for your health and lifestyle.
- Reverse your negative self-talk. If negative self-talk is an issue for you, you should make a conscious effort to stop this and reverse it. You simply alter the statement and repeat it to yourself, like an affirmation. For example, if your negative self-talk is telling you that you can't do something, tell yourself you can... *I can do [it]!* Repeat at least 10 times.

There are endless benefits of developing healthy habits, as this will certainly improve your health, and lifestyle, and reduce the anxiety symptoms in your life. It's the simple things in life that often have the biggest impact.

In the next chapter, we'll talk through how you can manage your anxiety in the long-term by planning. We'll consider what kind of planning you should be doing and how this can benefit you!

Chapter 8

Become a Planner

What does it mean to really become a planner?

We've talked about planning already in Chapter 6 when we considered your plan of attack. While it's important to create an initial plan to address your initial symptoms and triggers, it's important to plan for the long term too.

It's not always easy to take the time to consider your body, mind, and spirit when you have a busy life, but planning is the best way to continuously beat your anxiety. We've talked about creating a schedule already, and we've discussed how you can create an action plan to combat your anxiety, but when you're managing your anxiety, you need to make long-term plans so you can consistently overcome your triggers and symptoms with confidence.

In this chapter, we'll look at what kind of planning you should be doing at this stage of your journey, as well as talking through the benefits of planning and how you can begin to plan more, making it part of your life.

> *"You don't have to control your thoughts. You just have to stop letting them control you."*
>
> ~ Dan Millman

What Kind of Planning Should I Be Doing?

When you struggle with anxiety, it can be really difficult to recognize your own self-worth. Even though you've been working on recognizing and alleviating your anxiety triggers and symptoms, anxiety doesn't necessarily just go away.

It would be a mistake to stop working on your anxieties simply because you start to feel good and are getting better at how you handle it. Some people stop taking care of their needs because they believe they have eradicated their anxiety symptoms, but once they do this, they return, and they have to start again. To truly beat your anxiety symptoms, we need to understand it, and then put strategies in place to keep it under control—for good.

At this stage, the planning you should be doing should be aimed at helping you continue managing your anxiety symptoms in the long term. The schedule that you had when we discussed your plan of attack in Section 1, may need tweaking as you manage your anxiety better and move into the prevention stage. The good thing here is that you're going to establish a plan that helps you take care of yourself, while also being able to get on with your busy life.

This is exactly why planning is important... Because you have a life to live!

It's likely that you're already:

- Getting better at spotting your triggers
- Improving your anxiety by getting to the root cause
- Able to research your anxiety and remedy its symptoms
- Have steps in place to take care of your mind, body, and spirit

Which is fantastic. You're on fire, but... you need to keep going, and one way to do this is to become a planner.

If you plan and organize your month, then break it down into the week, then further into days, it helps you maintain your focus because you know what you're doing and when you're doing it.

Consider everything you do on a daily basis, a weekly basis, and a monthly basis and make lists correlating to that.

While a planner can act as a schedule, it isn't simply about writing down the things you need to do. Planning can help you:

- Get into a routine
- Set goals and focus on them
- Organize your time, so you get time with family and friends, as well as time to work, or relax
- Plan your day, so you know what to do and when
- Sort out your finances
- Monitor your sleep
- Record your anxiety episodes
- Prompt your memory

- Allows you to journal, so you can empty any thoughts in your head

And much, much more. Planning certainly helps you to manage the things that trigger your anxiety symptoms, while effectively managing your time, ensuring you create a better quality of life. While it may not eradicate your symptoms and triggers of anxiety completely, being a planner means you can manage it effectively.

Why is Planning Beneficial?

Being a good planner helps you melt away those symptoms. That's because you can write a schedule of what you need to do and when you need to do it. This reduces procrastination and helps to prompt your memory, and both of these things alleviate your anxiety symptoms.

Planning eases your anxiety symptoms because it helps you see your problems and allows you to put them into perspective. When we write down and take time to address the issues that have caused our anxiety, it's often not as bad as we think. Writing the information down can relieve the tension instantly.

Your focus can shift as you concentrate on possible solutions, rather than the problem and, as a result, your problem-solving skills get better which is an important life skill, especially when you're managing anxiety. Knowing what to do and when to do it helps you feel more in control of your life and gives you a feeling of hope.

When you begin to treat your anxiety, you will only be successful if you remove the fear from the relevant activities. We have a habit of only remembering the negative experiences we have in life, but keeping a journal or planner allows you to log the positive. You need to remember to positives, so start noting down the positive things each day.

Let's say you're nervous about speaking at an event, and you're drawn to the negatives. It's important to stop yourself and write down the positives from this experience.

What positives can come from speaking at an event?

Let's say you have to speak at the event, and this is causing you upset. While there are negatives to the experience that may be worrying you, there are also positives to take from the experience. When you speak at an event, you may be getting to share your story, your experience, or your knowledge—sometimes all three. The speaker would have made a leap towards overcoming their fears of speaking in a group, as well as improving their communication and presentation skills. This experience can therefore give you a sense of accomplishment too.

Moving on from this, you need to figure out your triggers and set goals to overcome your anxiety while you're planning. It's time to become more plan orientated.

How Can I Begin to Be More Plan-Oriented With My Life?

You should be living your best life; we all should. Planning is a learned skill, so it's not necessarily something that comes easily. But it is something we can adopt, but sometimes, it takes time.

Here are some top tips for building your long-term plan:

1. Make your vision clear – close your eyes and think about your ideal life. Consider all the things you want to accomplish, and what makes you happy. Think about the person you want to be, and also where you see yourself in a year, 5 years, or 10 years' time.
2. Create goals based on your vision – your goals should be practical, clear, and focused toward your vision. For that to be so, you should set SMART goals, i.e., specific, measurable, achievable, realistic, and time bound. Your goals should relate to your career or education, family, your home life, and your overall well-being.
3. Work with what you already have - take your previous plan of attack and schedule from Chapter 6 and compare it with the visions and goals you've just produced. Pull out what things you believe are relevant when it comes to your vision and goals. If you've developed a schedule already that suits you, work from that, and tweak it as necessary. You may consider keeping your exercise routine, your affirmations, and meditations in the morning or evening if you feel they are helping you and will continue to help you in the long-term.
4. Identify any recurring anxieties or those that you're currently controlling – when exploring your plan of attack, you need to identify your recurring anxieties and the anxieties that you're currently keeping under control. Consider how they fit into your plan. If the symptoms have improved, you may want to be wary about them, but you may not need to focus on them as much as you did when they were a bigger problem.

5. Create or buy a planner – decide if you want one or multiple. Some people decide to keep one planner for them personally, that looks at their career, education, and personal well-being, with another that concentrates on their family and home life. Others prefer to keep only one planner that logs everything.
6. Check your plan - ensure your plan caters to your:
    a. Career or education wants and needs
    b. Family life, including your kids, parents, and other family members or responsibilities you have
    c. Home life, including financial responsibilities
    d. Overall well-being, which looks at your mind, body, and spirit
7. Start living it! If you want to start living your best life, start following and implementing your plan. Make sure you follow every aspect and take care of yourself, as well as being constantly aware of your triggers, symptoms, and anxiety. This includes being aware of any new anxiety symptoms if you are faced with any.

If you have a schedule and your goals are written down for you to refer to every day, you'll find that you're spending more time maintaining your focus on achieving your goals, rather than focusing on your anxious feelings.

When you plan, your life becomes so much easier, and when life takes an unexpected turn that's beyond your control, there's nothing much you can do. Even when life is busy, you should always schedule time for yourself. We'll talk about that next.

Chapter 9

Take Time for Yourself

Many people view "Me Time" negatively, but the truth is, it can have a very positive influence on your life. "Me time" is often viewed as being self-indulgent and selfish, but research suggests that those who engage regularly in high-quality "me time" are more productive at work. Those who invest time in themselves are often more successful in life, because taking time for yourself shows you value who you are.

> *"It is hard to love yourself if you never spend time with yourself. 'Alone Time' is necessary."*
>
> ~ *Izey Victoria Odiase*

One of the biggest resistances against "me time" is that you don't have the time to waste. You're always going to have the negative self-talk in your ear telling you that you don't have time to spend time on you, but if you want to make the best of your life, it's the most valuable thing you can do. "Me time" is an asset. In this chapter, we'll talk through the different ways to incorporate "me time" into your busy life.

We're also going to talk about the importance of taking time for yourself, as well as discussing the different things you can do during this time. We'll also consider how much time you should commit to "me time" and how this can improve aspects of your life, while also linking to how this can improve your anxiety.

What Kind of Things Should I Take Time to Do for Myself?

You have an important decision to make...

How much time can you commit each day to yourself?

It's recommended that you take between 30-60 minutes daily for yourself, however, if you've been neglecting yourself, giving this amount of time each day to yourself could set your teeth on edge. If this is the case and you feel you can only spare 15 minutes each day, for now, start off by committing to that. Once you start to recognize the benefits of "me time," you can increase this slowly, until you get to 30 minutes "me time," or even better, 60 minutes every day.

Believe it or not, if you manage your time effectively and continue to set goals, you'll find that you have more time. Taking time for yourself has many benefits, but the main benefit includes reducing your levels of anxiety.

There are many things you can do when you take time just for you. Some people prefer to sit alone and reflect, read, sleep, or spend time in nature. Just make sure you're doing something for you. Something you enjoy.

Here are 20 "me time" ideas to get you started:

Take Time for Yourself

1. Take a bath – why not light some candles, put on some relaxing music, and run a bath? Be sure to lock the door and inform your family that you shouldn't be interrupted if necessary.
2. Read a magazine or a book – kick back and relax, while reading your favorite magazine or book.
3. Take a walk – get yourself outdoors. Walking is great exercise, and it can also help you feel refreshed and rejuvenated.
4. Learn a new skill – we never stop learning, so take some time to develop yourself by learning a new skill.
5. Book "me time" into your diary – it's an appointment with yourself, so treat it like one. Don't disappoint yourself by missing it.
6. Breathe and meditate – you already know the benefits of breathing and meditating, so if you're not doing this, you should consider giving it a go. It's all about you!
7. Take a tech break – turn off your cell and be silent. It's okay to be alone with your own mind.
8. Give yourself a facial – you can take some time for a little pampering at home. Wash your face first, and then apply a facial scrub. Then, steam your face by placing a towel over your head, over a hot bowl, and then put on a face or mud mask. Remove the mask, and then moisturize.
9. Take a shopping trip – every once in a while, you deserve a treat. Treat yourself. Go shopping for a new outfit that makes you feel great.
10. Treat yourself to a latte – while many of us are watching what we spend, if you have the money, you

can certainly reward yourself with a latte from your favorite coffee shop on occasion.

11. Take a nap – *what better way to spend your "me time" than taking a nap?* If you have a busy life, it's normal to feel tired. When you have your "me time," there's no reason why you can't take a nap too. Ten to 20 minutes can make such a difference to some people as they can certainly boost your energy levels.

12. Take an exercise class – exercise is great at boosting your energy levels and can leave you feeling fabulous. It can also increase your physical fitness too.

13. Book a spa break – if you have the money, you should certainly spend it on a spa break. This is the ultimate way to relax and unwind. If this isn't possible for you right now, why not recreate a spa at home (just like the facial in point 8, but add some other treatments too).

14. Go for a swim – swimming is a great way to spend your alone time. It will help you stay fit, but it's also refreshing. It's a great way to unwind, while also boosting your energy levels.

15. Coloring for adults – coloring can distract you and help you spend enjoyable time alone. You should certainly give this a try, especially if you're the creative type.

16. Call a friend – talking to our friends about life in general and spending time catching up is a great way to spend your alone time. Talking about what's going on in your life is really therapeutic, so it will help both you and your friend.

17. Take up a hobby – reconnect with yourself and consider the things you enjoy doing or would like to

do for fun. When you've decided on a hobby, take it up and enjoy.

18. Do a puzzle – this is great for the mind, as it's a great visual exercise and helps you to solve problems effectively.
19. Join a club – if there's something you like doing, it's likely that there's a club related to that hobby. Whether it's a book club, a science fiction club, a cooking on a budget club, or a sports club, you'll get to hang out with like-minded people doing something you love.
20. Take up rock climbing – if you like a thrill and want a challenge, take up something that requires strength and resilience like rock climbing. If you've got the grit, you won't regret it.

There are so many things you can do as part of your alone time, so really consider the things you like to do or the things you most want to do. Maybe you want to go rock climbing in the Grand Canyon. If you want that, then you can set goals detailing when you can get there.

"Me time" is extremely important, and we're going to talk about this next. In the meantime, make a promise to yourself right now...

Whatever activities you choose as part of your "me time," promise that you'll embrace and enjoy them...

Why is it Important That I Have *Me Time*?

Life is busy. It can be difficult to focus on yourself without feeling a sense of guilt, however, if you want to take care of others and have responsibilities in life, taking care of yourself is really important. We've discussed caring for your mind, body, and spirit, and "me time" can be a big part of this. It helps you regain control over your life and when you invest time in yourself, you're placing value on yourself. Having alone time helps you review and assess your life, but it also allows you the time to reconnect with your vision and goals and listen to your inner self.

"Me time" allows you to get clear headspace to think things through and reflect on your life, which can bring you a lot of clarity. It means you can make decisions in everyday life, which may require negotiations and compromise. This is because it allows you time to consider the best way to respond or act in certain situations without feeling guilty. Alone time allows you time to reconnect with yourself and do the things you love in life, the things that bring you joy. Making time for your hobbies gives you a sense of your life being worth living. If you have something to look forward to, working towards that goal can reduce anxiety.

While there is only guidance regarding the amount of time you should spend on your "me time," you should ensure you take enough time out to impact you. You should feel recharged and refreshed, and ready to take on the day ahead.

"Me time" provides you with a time of contemplation. It reboots your brain, improves your concentration, it helps you unwind, provides you with an opportunity for self-discovery, and it can enhance relationships in your life.

It also helps you to become more self-aware, manage and contemplate inner conflicts, and improve your problem-solving abilities while also making you more productive. Overall, it can help you rediscover who you are and encourage self-love. All of these things improve your life, boost your self-esteem and confidence, and aid you on your journey to happiness and harmony.

How Can I Fit *Me Time* Into My Busy Life?

The most common excuse for neglecting "me time" is not being able to find the time. In order to introduce this into your life, you need to make it as simple as possible. It's up to you to find a way around this excuse, but there are some hacks you can use to try and fit in this valuable activity:

1. Take your lunch outside and eat on the terrace at work
2. Take a walk during your break
3. Unplug your tech gadgets
4. Wake up 30 minutes earlier than your family
5. Organize and declutter your home

Your "me time" is going to be most beneficial if it's undisturbed, so you may need to assert the reasons why you're spending time alone. The best way to approach this is by:

- Being direct and honest by explaining to your family and friends that you need to rejuvenate the mind and body by having some "me time."

- Explain to your partner and other family members why me time is important to you, and how it helps you emotionally. You should also talk about how happy it makes you.

- Encourage others to have their own "me time" too and respect their space.

- If you have a partner, take some time together as a couple too.
- If you don't have time to spend each day, assign a free night each week, or a weekend every few months to spend on your hobby or with like-minded people.

If there's something you're particularly looking forward to doing, create a goal for doing this, but then create smaller steps and tick off your progress as you head towards your goal. Monitoring your progress ensures you stay motivated and focused as you head toward your goal.

Taking time for you allows you to enjoy your life while also keeping your anxiety symptoms at bay. Life is there for living, so while you're taking time to care for yourself, you should make the most of it and get some enjoyment from the things you do.

You deserve happiness and enjoyment, so be sure to plan this into your schedule!

Chapter 10

It's All About Perspective

You're still working on beating your anxiety symptoms, and you're already doing great. You'll have heard the term perspective time and time again, but it can be hard to intuit what perspective means. Your perspective is your attitude and point of view in relation to something else.

Your anxiety symptoms can warp the way you perceive things in your life!

When we began Section 2, we looked at your plan of action, your mind, body, and spirit, and considered your mindset in Chapter 8, , before we moved on to how you can spend time on yourself, without feeling guilty. You've made excellent progress so far as we head into the final chapter of Section 2, and here, we're going to focus on spirit again, while also referring to purposeful lifestyles.

In order to do that, you must have the right perspective on life. It's not always easy to understand, but perspective is relative. It's time to talk about what perspective really means...

> *"We can complain because rose bushes have thorns, or rejoice because thorns have roses."*
>
> ~ Alphonse Karr

What's your perspective; will you complain or rejoice?

What Does "It's All About Perspective" Mean?

Your perspective is formed on your feelings, emotions, thoughts, desires, opinions, and beliefs. It's subjective, which means it's not necessarily factual unless we already have the belief that something is true. Your perspective is ultimately how you perceive something; it is how you see it!

But you can control how you perceive things...

Anxiety is something that can alter our perspective in a negative way. Those who allow the negative influences to alter their perspective are the 'complainers' mentioned in the quote above; they complain because the rose bush has thorns.

To beat your anxiety, you must constantly work on changing or challenging your mindset and belief systems. You should aim to be more positive when it comes to your perspective which means you should aim to have a more positive outlook. As the quote above indicates, a person with a more positive thinking pattern would choose to rejoice because the thorns have pretty roses.

Now we know what perspective means, it's time to address the question posed in this chapter...

What does "It's all about perspective" mean?

It's All About Perspective

It's all about perspective means the angle from which you view your life. Our feelings, beliefs, and experiences form the lens of how we see the world, but we don't often see things for what they are. This is specific to you, and your perspective shapes how you view your life and the things you do.

If you're sticking to your plan, you will be exercising and eating well, and if you're staying organized in your life, it's likely you'll feel a sense of fulfillment and accomplishment. When it comes to taking time for yourself or taking part in your hobby, you should certainly feel a sense of enjoyment for that. You should certainly feel fulfilled. If this is you, it sounds like your anxiety is under control and you're in a good place. You have a positive mindset, which means you are more likely to have a positive perception of the world.

If you perceive things in a more positive way, you'll find that your anxiety levels will plummet, and you will become more confident. The way you perceive your life can ultimately impact your anxiety because it lessens its intensity.

Why is the Way I Perceive Life Important?

Our perspective helps us make informed decisions and problem-solve. It also encourages us to focus on the positive things in life and it helps us identify the things that we don't need to waste our time on.

Our mindset impacts how we approach life in general, and this can vary. If we feel good, are managing our symptoms of anxiety, and are enjoying aspects of our life, anxiety is low risk. If we're not having a great time right now and our anxiety is trying to break out, our perspective can be distorted, which means we are not always capable of making the right decisions. Our outlook on life will be distorted and we're more likely to take a more negative view.

* Consider how your perspective influences the way you manage your anxiety, in fact, it's recommended that you keep a journal regarding this (some of you may be keeping one already). Be sure to detail the things you've done, and the progress you've made.

*Reflect on your progress and how far you've come.

Anxiety impacts our emotional state, and if our emotional state is impacted, it can be difficult to interact with the world and make positive choices. It means we're distracted and have trouble concentrating on tasks. That's because it's difficult to stay motivated; negativity is draining!

How Can This Ultimately Reduce My Anxiety?

Perspective matters. When you're under stress or pressure, the brain automatically switches focus on the negatives, rather than the positives. You've been working throughout Section 2 to change the way you view anxiety, and your perspective plays a huge part in this. It ultimately influences the way you deal with your anxiety symptoms.

Eventually, your perspective reduces your level of anxiety, as if you have a positive perspective, it brings you a feeling of hope and allows you to make positive and logical decisions. If you're enjoying life and are doing the

It's All About Perspective

things you enjoy, then it's likely that you feel fulfilled. This means that your anxiety will likely be at a lower level.

* *Use your journal to reflect on your progress so far.*

Having a positive perspective means you are embracing positive thinking and there are many ways in which it remedies your anxiety. For example:

1. Positive thinking puts a lid on negative self-talk which reduces the stress in your life. This has a domino effect because less negative self-talk reduces stress, and they both lower the intensity of your anxiety symptoms.
2. There are many health benefits to positive thinking. This includes having lower rates of depression, stress, and pain, having a greater resilience against illness, and better coping skills during times of stress, to name a few. Depression, stress, pain, lack of coping skills, and low resilience rates can all be triggers and causes of anxiety.
3. It allows you to identify areas of your life for development, which means you're willing to grow and develop as a person. Having a mindset and attitude that strives towards growth often links to feelings of happiness.
4. It encourages you to embrace the things you love in life. A positive attitude won't allow you to make excuses as to why you can't take time for yourself. Putting things into perspective and accepting that you should have time just for you provides you with feelings of enjoyment and fulfillment, which alleviates your feelings of anxiety.

In Section 3, we'll talk about overcoming your anxiety, which means we'll learn how to face it and tackle it head-on. Just before we move into the next section of this book, it's important to strengthen your feelings on perspective.

Activity

For this activity, you may need to refer to your journal. If you haven't kept a journal yet, keep one over the next week and ensure you're noting down your perspective and consider if it's positive or negative (maybe it's both, but what patterns do you notice):

*Consider your perspectives

*What negative perspectives are a recurring pattern for you?

*How can you challenge these perspectives?

You've successfully reached the end of Section 2, which means, you're likely managing your anxiety symptoms well. Now you're ready to begin overcoming your anxieties, for good. You're making steady progress, so keep going. As we head into Section 3, we'll talk through overcoming some of the most common forms of anxiety.

> *"Anxiety was born in the very same moment as mankind. And since we will never be able to master it, we will have to learn to live with it—just as we have learned to live with storms."*
>
> ~ *Paulo Coelho*

Section 3: Overcoming Your Anxiety

Chapter 11

Facing Anxiety from Responsibility

You are obviously anxious for a reason, and in Section 3, we're going to explore the most common types of anxiety and discover how you can approach them. We'll talk about anxieties in the home, as a worker or leader, or even as a student, as anxiety is something that you may need to face at different points in your life.

Don't worry, you'll be prepared to handle any anxiety symptoms that you're faced with!

Sometimes, anxiety can happen because you fear your responsibilities, or you may even fear that you neglect your responsibilities. Fearing your responsibilities is actually a common form of anxiety and is known as hypengyophobia, and this is the first type of anxiety we're going to consider as it's more important than ever to conquer this fear.

In this chapter, we're going to explore what exactly hypengyophobia is and the most common root causes of this fear. We're also going to explore why it's important to conquer this fear, and how you can begin to do this.

Before we begin, you should reflect on the quote below:

> *"Nothing in life is to be feared. It is only to be understood."*
>
> ~ Marie Curie

What is Hypengyophobia?

It's been mentioned already that hypengyophobia is the fear of your responsibility, but it's a little more complex than that. Those who suffer with this phobia must recognize that, like most phobias, their fear is irrational.

When something we feel is irrational, it's an intense feeling, however, while we may believe it, it's not logical or reasonable. It can be difficult to take a step back and realize that the way we are feeling is out there. As the anxiety builds, it can set off a panic attack, although this doesn't happen in every instance.

When a person has hypengyophobia, they may find that they do what they can to avoid the thing or things they fear. When you find you're worrying excessively, your irrational thinking can escalate, and this can lead to mental turmoil. Avoiding the responsibilities you fear will not resolve your issues and, therefore, they will continue to escalate.

Hypengyophobia is often caused by a lack of confidence, a fear of failure, and a lack of feeling in control. This type of anxiety commonly exists in both your work and home life, and it can create conflict with your peers. You may also find you are battling with your mind too.

It's easy to spot some phobias, especially if you find you fear a specific object, but if you fear something less concrete, like responsibilities, it's not as easy to notice. If you have hypengyophobia, anxiety is a key symptom, but you'll notice that you're struggling to cope with this, and sometimes this results in a panic attack too. You could find that you're regularly avoiding responsibilities and you could also suffer from sweating, muscle tension, and you could even shake as a result.

There are no specific known causes of hypengyophobia, which can make this even more difficult to identify. Those with specific phobias or mental illness within their family history could be more at risk of developing this, so it's certainly something you should consider. Your environment can also play a part in developing hypengyophobia. For instance, if a person has suffered from a traumatic event in which has impacted how they view responsibilities or the idea of having responsibilities, they could be at risk of developing hypengyophobia as a result. For example, if they were neglected as a child, it may impact how they view parenthood or relationships.

Why is it Important to Conquer this Fear?

It's important to conquer hypengyophobia because if you don't, you'll continue to shirk your responsibilities. If you do this, you're giving up your power to grow because progressing in life often means being held accountable for your decisions or actions.

Taking on responsibilities helps you take ownership of your education, your life, and your career, as it shows you're in command of these things. If you avoid responsibilities, you'll find that you stagnate, which can lead to further issues. This is because your hypengyophobia will escalate as it's left unidentified and untreated. The longer this goes on, the more difficult it becomes to overcome.

As humans, most of us have a need to grow and progress and with this comes responsibility, and there are many advantages to this. If you are dealing with symptoms of anxiety when it comes to responsibility, the first thing you must remember is that YOU are in control of your life!

Hypengyophobia often means you relinquish control of your life. It's important to recognize that you have a choice. It's up to you if you want to take up a certain responsibility, and if you decide not to, that is your decision. On the flip side, that also means it's your decision if you choose to take up this responsibility. It's important to see that both failure and success from responsibility hangs on you, and that's a good thing, it's not a negative.

If you don't conquer this fear, you will miss out on opportunities to grow and it's unlikely you'll be able to move forward with your own pursuits. While many people believe life is easier without responsibility, this is a superficial notion as it actually makes life more difficult due to its many disadvantages. Those who do conquer this fear become better problem-solvers and are open to learning and growing, meaning their life is leading towards success.

Whether we care to admit it or not, responsibility is a part of life, so it's something that everyone has to accept. Starting off small is a bigger step than you may think.

Simply accepting it's your responsibility to take action is a huge step for you to take. *Commit to taking action right now. Read the next section so you can begin to overcome your hypengyophobia.*

How Can I Begin to Overcome Hypengyophobia?

Overcoming your fears is an opportunity for you to grow, even though you don't see it yet. From every failure, we learn, and as we progress, we get to reap the rewards of success. While there are several treatment paths to choose from, there is no treatment that is specifically designed for this condition. It's important, therefore, to treat the symptoms as this will significantly improve how you feel about your fear.

Let's consider four of these methods including exposure therapy, CBT, DBT, and Yoga.

1. Exposure Therapy – this treatment is one of the most common for people who have a phobia. It basically means you're exposed to your phobias, slowly, in a controlled way and have a plan on how to deal with this or respond. The aim of exposure therapy is to help you build up a tolerance to your fears which, over time, desensitizes you to the impact they have on you.

2. Cognitive Behavior Therapy (CBT) – this treatment is often used to treat anxiety symptoms. It can be a great treatment for those who are suffering from hypengyophobia, as a therapist can help you discover why you are feeling, thinking, or behaving in a particular way regarding your fear, so you can start altering your approach towards this. It helps you start

to identify when you're hypengyophobia is triggered, so you can take a step back and analyze them in-depth before learning how to deal with them. Awareness is often the first step towards overcoming.

3. Dialectical Behavior Therapy (DBT) - this treatment focuses on regulating your emotions, so that you can learn to cope with your anxiety. DBT is generally a 6-month long group session and although it's focused on people who suffer with anxiety disorders and borderline personality disorder, it is an effective treatment for those who suffer from hypengyophobia too. You will use techniques such as half-smiling, and mindfulness meditation to switch your focus, deal with your emotions, and clear your mind.

4. Yoga for hypengyophobia – yoga is a great treatment for anxiety symptoms in general and it is a key mindfulness practice. Yoga can be extremely beneficial for those who suffer from hypengyophobia, as it helps to relieve some of the anxiety you feel by directing your focus and attention towards something more productive. There are so many different types of yoga, such as hatha, kundalini, and laughter yoga, but almost every type in existence can help when it comes to the anxiety that is linked with hypengyophobia. Yoga is something you can practice on your own as there are many free videos out there that can help you get started, however, if you've never done this before, going to a class can be beneficial in the beginning.

Sometimes, a doctor will prescribe medication to help ease the symptoms of your hypengyophobia if they believe it is helpful to you. You may be prescribed antidepressants or anti-anxiety medications, as they

Facing Anxiety from Responsibility

can reduce symptoms of anxiety and can prevent panic attacks. Some medication needs to be taken daily, while others do not. Make sure you speak to your doctor and follow their instructions as they will determine the best course of action for you.

Other things can help with hypengyophobia, such as reducing caffeine, increasing your cardio exercise, and using meditation techniques, so it's worth considering these things as a course of action.

In life, it's normal for us to encounter conflict and uncomfortable situations, so it's important you learn to embrace this. Taking on responsibilities is a challenge, but it prepares you for the future. Life is a journey, and whether you fail or succeed at everything, it's all part of your journey. If you don't put in the effort or at least try, you'll never make any progress.

We learn by things we don't succeed in instantly, so if you're struggling to take on responsibility, take it slow. Take on smaller responsibilities that increase over time, as this will help to alleviate your anxiety symptoms. Put in the time to prepare for your new responsibilities by researching, and ask others to help or give you guidance, so you can build up your confidence when it comes to managing your responsibilities. If you go the extra mile, you will certainly conquer your fear!

Chapter 12

Facing Anxiety in Relationships

Throughout our lives, we encounter many different relationships. We have relationships with coworkers at work, with our family and friends, and we have romantic relationships. We also form relationships with acquaintances, such as neighbors or people we see regularly in the community but are not necessarily friends with. Sometimes, relationships can cause us to experience symptoms of anxiety.

In this chapter, we're going to clarify exactly what relationship anxiety is, while also talking about why it's important to deal with this type of anxiety and its symptoms. We're also going to focus on how you can practice overcoming relationship anxiety too.

Let's learn to identify and overcome relationship anxiety, for good!

What is Relationship Anxiety?

Relationship anxiety is another common form of anxiety, and it presents itself in a variety of ways. Someone who believes they suffer from relationship anxiety may find they question themselves about the relationships they've formed with others even though they've already established boundaries and developed trust.

A person who has relationship anxiety often doubts the relationship and may:

- Believe they are incapable of maintaining healthy relationships with others
- Worry about whether things will last or not
- Feel insecure about the relationship and wonder if it's a relationship they should or should not be in

The doubts they experience often spiral because if you have relationship anxiety, you can find you're constantly in doubt, which means the relationships in your life are affected and you could even find yourself believing that the other person in the relationship is out to get you. Of course, there are many ways in which it can present itself and even if the relationship is going well, the person may have anxiety by:

1. Doubting whether the other person in the relationship even likes them
2. Feeling unable to open up or be themselves around the other person
3. Believing they are not good enough to have a relationship with the other person
4. Overreacting or overthinking the simple or normal situations that present themselves during the relationship

Yet, surprisingly, relationship anxiety is extremely common. Whether it's between you and your friends, boss, coworkers, family, or even in a romantic capacity, relationship anxiety means that one of the people in the relationship has anxious feelings and if this is not dealt with, it can lead to emotional distress, an upset stomach or other physical issues, emotional exhaustion or fatigue, and lack of motivation. One important thing to remember when it comes to relationship anxiety is that it often doesn't stem from the relationship itself, however, if it is not dealt with effectively, it can cause relationship issues and distress for both parties.

So, if it's not the relationship itself that causes relationship anxiety, you're probably wondering what does. Well, it can be a number of issues, which are often linked to your feelings and emotions, and it can even be in reference to how you feel about yourself. Feeling insecure about the relationship, particularly in the early stages, when you can find it difficult to build up trust or are worried about commitment is a common point in time of when relationship anxiety first occurs.

Relationship anxiety can cause you to question your relationship, for instance, you may think:

- How much do I mean to the person I'm in a relationship with, or do I even matter to them at all?
- What does the other person get from our relationship?
- Does the other person really love or like me?
- Does the other person want to break up or fall out with me?
- Does the other person even value our friendship/relationship?
- Are we even compatible enough to have a relationship?

If you're questioning yourself in a similar way, and doubting your relationships, it could mean you have relationship anxiety. This has a knock-on effect as it can then cause you to sabotage the relationship.

When relationship anxiety spirals, we can find ourselves in a position in which we sabotage the relationship, as we feel we are protecting ourselves by doing this. If you find yourself picking arguments, pushing others away while insisting there's nothing wrong, or pushing the boundaries of your relationship by deliberately doing things to annoy the other person, then it's likely you're already beginning to unintentionally sabotage your relationship/s.

Obviously, if you don't deal with your anxiety, you will ultimately push others away. This leads us into our next, important section... *Why is it so important to deal with our relationship anxiety?*

Why is it Important to Deal With This?

If you don't work on or prevent your relationship anxiety, it can be difficult to progress in life as your relationships are a key aspect of your life. You're basically sabotaging the opportunities you have throughout your life, and it can make you miserable. If your relationship anxiety escalates, you'll struggle; it can impair your ability to communicate and trust, and it also influences your behavior as you can become very irrational. It would be impossible to enter a long-term, loving relationship, further your career, or grow as a person if you cannot effectively maintain the relationships in your life.

When you worry about the relationships in your life, it can cause you to experience feelings of loneliness. This is because of the distance you create between yourself and others, and the barriers you place in between. This is because your anxiety causes you to think negatively, and as a result of that, you act or behave irrationally, which eventually pushes the people you love away.

Many people who have relationship anxiety become clingy and controlling; they try to punish others in some way or respond aggressively; and they can reject others or withhold their feelings from their partner. They can even find themselves retreating and taking the attitude that they should give up on relationships entirely.

This obviously isn't healthy!

People with relationship anxiety often try to use techniques of sabotage to determine how much the other person in the relationship cares or values it, but the problem is, it often has the opposite impact and pushes them away. It's important to consider this in context... Other people cannot determine why you're reacting this way, especially if they are unaware that you have relationship anxiety.

Overthinking situations can mean you're making a problem when there really isn't one. Basically, your overthinking causes you to jump to conclusions without any evidence. For example, if your boss cancels the meeting you were supposed to be having regarding your promotion, it doesn't mean that they don't want to promote you because they don't like you. There could be a number of reasons because, when you're in a leadership role, you have to prioritize your responsibilities, so maybe something urgent came up or maybe it was a personal issue that they don't wish to disclose. If you jump to conclusions and react as a result, your behavior that follows could mean you sabotage your opportunities.

Of course, as with any anxiety symptoms, this could mean you suffer from further issues in the future. You could find that you become depressed, and you may find it difficult to communicate with others, which can also damage your self-esteem.

While you probably realize the severity of relationship anxiety if it's allowed to escalate, it's time to focus on the main causes of relationship anxiety and how you can overcome it.

You can build better relationships, for life!

How Can I Practice Overcoming Relationship Anxiety?

The key to overcoming relationship anxiety is figuring out what caused it in the first place. Identifying such things can take time and you must be dedicated to exploring these in detail but getting to the root of the matter can be difficult.

Your past experiences can affect you, even if you believe you've moved on. If someone previously left you, lied to you, cheated on you, misled you, or mistreated you in some way, they will have hurt you and it can cause you to doubt others as a result. While you may enter a relationship with good intentions, you may find that certain behaviors trigger you as they remind you of the past, which can provoke you to start doubting them and invoke feelings of insecurity.

The first relationships we form are with our parents or caregivers when we're babies or young children. We grow attached to them and if they meet our needs when it comes to love and support, we'll feel secure. If your needs are not met as a child, insecurities can stem from childhood. If you are unable to identify the root cause of your relationship anxiety, it's worth considering that it's possible that this stems from your childhood, which means you could have anxiety symptoms when it comes to expressing how you feel and committing to the relationship you have with others.

Other causes of relationship anxiety can be due to low self-esteem or an incessant need to doubt yourself by questioning all your decisions. When we have low self-esteem, it can cause us to feel insecure in our relationships and can leave us doubting how others feel about us. This is because you project how you feel onto others, and if you're already feeling low about yourself, it can be difficult to imagine that others value you. Let's say you've responded in a particular way and have upset someone, which makes you feel angry with yourself. You may feel that the person is angry with you too and you may even feel this is justified because you're angry with yourself. If you often question yourself regarding your choices and decisions, it can be a healthy sign, as it means you take the time you need to consider your choices. If you're filled with self-doubt and you find that you often get stuck in an incessant pattern of questions that encourage you to doubt everything, it soon becomes an issue.

This doesn't serve you; it's not productive!

The good news, you can overcome this...

To do so, you should:

1. Pinpoint why you feel like this – *what's driving your anxiety?* We've explored different ways of evaluating your anxiety in Section 1 of this book (chapters 3-6) so dig deep and get to the root cause.
2. Be open and honest when it comes to your feelings – while you may find it difficult to express how you feel, it's important to communicate how you feel to others. A relationship, regardless of type, works both ways, and being honest can actually strengthen relationships. Start small, and don't be afraid to tell the other person if you struggle to let others know how you feel. You'll often find they're supportive.
3. Build-up the trust – this leads on from the previous tip, because if you start to be open and honest with others, you'll begin to build trust in your relationships, and this means you're building healthy connections. Trust takes time, but it's essential.
4. Listen to what others have to say – don't shut down others when they have listened to you. Communication works both ways, so if you're going to express your point or feelings to them, listen to their points too. Make a conscious effort to listen and it will soon become a habit.
5. Use techniques to calm yourself down when feelings of anxiety rise – you've already been exploring different ways to calm your anxiety levels. Things like deep or controlled breathing, meditation, yoga, or exercise can all be used to soothe your anxiety. You may have even figured out some other ways of doing this too. Figure out which self-soothe method works best against your relationship anxiety symptoms by

trying them out. Sometimes, simply calming your mind and refocusing allows you to put things into perspective.

6. Accept yourself – we've talked about self-acceptance, and this is extremely important when it comes to relationship anxiety. Your feelings are valid, and whilst they may not always be a fact, you're still feeling it. If you're struggling to accept who you are or accept your feelings, you may need to commence work on your self-esteem. Take a step back, acknowledge how you feel, accept it, then put it into perspective. Imagine your friend feels this way and you're giving them advice, *what would you tell them?*

7. Address the issue – if there is conflict in your relationship, you do need to address it; otherwise, you risk a relationship breakdown. Make sure you take responsibility for your part in the conflict and focus on expressing how you feel as this may help you get to the root of the matter. Remember to listen to your partner too!

8. Do not devalue yourself and others – you are worthy. You deserve to be treated well, so make sure you can differentiate between relationship anxiety and anxiety that is caused because others are not treating you well. Everyone should appreciate you for who you are, and you should respond in the same way towards others.

9. Express appreciation to the supportive people in your life – consider who the most supportive people are in your life and express your gratitude towards them. Showing gratitude increases the emotional connection you have with others and improves your

ability to respond positively. In fact, your life may be more positive as a result. If others impact your life in a positive way, *why not acknowledge this and let them know how grateful you are?*

Improving your relationships can have a deeper impact on your life. Your communication skills will get better and will improve personally as in your education and career. Strong relationships ultimately lead to success!

In the next chapter, we're going to focus on another common anxiety that comes with public speaking. It's likely there'll be a time in your life when you're asked to do this, so the sooner you overcome this, the better.

It's time to drop the mic!

Chapter 13

Facing Anxiety When Speaking

If you feel anxious about speaking in public, you're certainly not alone. Trust me, everyone feels it; this is a normal reaction!

When we speak in public, this can sometimes be on a small-scale, such as speaking at meetings with only five people in attendance, or it can be on a much larger scale, such as talking in front of a massive crowd. Many professional speakers have admitted to feeling anxious before a speaking event, even if they've done this successfully on numerous occasions.

In this chapter, we're going to talk about speaking anxiety, and consider what you can do if you become anxious but MUST speak. We'll also talk about why it's so important to overcome this fear, as well as discussing how you can become a better speaker while keeping your speaking anxiety under control.

Are you ready to disentangle your speaking anxiety?

What Do I Do if I Become Anxious and Have to Speak?

It's not easy to jump in front of a group of people and speak. Common anxiety symptoms before a speaking event often include physical reactions such as sweating, fidgeting, or shaking. That's because to some people, speaking feels like a scary thing and many people who talk about their fear of speaking often put this down to fear, such as being judged or criticized by their audience, while others blame imposter syndrome.

The truth is, speaking in public puts you on the spot. You are in the limelight, and this can be overwhelming as you can feel instant pressure. If you must speak and have a sudden surge of anxiousness, there are some things you can do to try and alleviate some speaking pressure:

1. Don't try to be perfect – the people listening to you will only be inspired if you're natural. Our imperfections make us unique, relatable, and real, so don't see speaking as a way to impress, see it as a way to show the real you and this way, your audience will learn to trust you.

2. Use your anxiety for the greater good – we've talked about 'good' anxiety already and this applies here too. If you're anxious about something, it often means you care, but those feelings can also cause your adrenaline to kick in which means your senses are heightened. This means you can often speak fluently, think fast, and even be more determined or enthusiastic, so you perform better.

3. Prepare in advance – if you're speaking to a group of people, it's likely that you'll get plenty of notice, so

ensure you are clear when it comes to your subject matter and create a list of engaging questions that will hold your audience's attention.
4. Use visualization techniques – the best way to prevent your anxiety symptoms from spiraling is to visualize your success. See yourself delivering your speech with confidence. Imagine the room and the people, and even imagine you and how you look. Think about the best possible outcome from the event and also consider how you can turn this vision into reality.
5. Don't forget to breathe – just before the event, you should practice deep breathing. This will help you to clear your mind and resume your focus. It will reduce some of the pressure you feel regarding your public speaking.

If you have a speaking gig, or have a job opportunity that involves speaking, you should be working towards any fears you have regarding speaking.

*Create a brain dump based on the following question – *When you imagine speaking in public, what negative thoughts and fears spring to mind?*

Knowing what you're actually afraid of when it comes to speaking can be the key to overcoming it. Crushing your speaking anxiety symptoms is extremely important, and now it's time to reflect on why that is...

Why is it Important to Crush This Fear?

It's extremely important to crush your speaking fear because it can prevent you from taking opportunities when it comes to your career. Ask yourself:

- What if you have the opportunity of promotion in your job, but it requires speaking?
- What if your career path takes you on a journey toward public speaking?

As mentioned earlier, people often fear public speaking as they don't want to be criticized or judged, but when we put this in perspective... You have been asked or chosen to do this because others believe you're the right person to do it.

The fear of speaking in public will hold you back because it's likely that at some point in your life (whether you expect it to or not), you'll be required to speak in public. The longer you allow the fear to fester, the more difficult it is to overcome, so ask yourself this: *Are you going to allow your fear of speaking to hold you back?*

You cannot allow this fear to dictate your life, as you should not be in a position in which you're turning down opportunities in order to avoid speaking. You are in control of your own destiny, so take back the control and work to overcome this fear.

Don't let it control you!

How Can I Become a Better Speaker and Remove This Anxiety?

There are many ways to become a better speaker and the better you get at speaking, the more likely it is that your symptoms of anxiety will improve. When you're speaking to a group of people, you should always ensure you:

- Know your topic well – it's likely you already do if you're speaking about it.

- Be organized – plan out your presentation or speech ahead of time and get any props you need ready. You could also time your speech, so you know you can stick to the schedule.

- Keep practicing, once or twice isn't enough – if you really want to be prepared to speak, you need to practice over and over again. You should do it in front of a mirror first, and then in front of friends or family, before practicing to a smaller audience if possible. Consider videoing or recording this too, so you can make judgements yourself of how to improve.

- Make sure you practice keeping your composure and using body language – doing this adds character and feeling to your speech and can make the presentation more engaging as it shows how passionate you are when it comes to your topic. This often keeps the audience's attention.

- Write yourself little positive notes – this could be points of encouragement and development points, so you know how to improve. Ensure you write yourself plenty of encouragement notes though!

- Challenge your concerns – ask yourself what you're really afraid of when it comes to your speaking worries and note them down. Challenge them directly; *what's the worst that can happen as a result of your concern? Why do you think this is a worry to you? Is it a valid concern or worry?*

- Don't fear the silence – silence is often a good thing. If you pose a question to your audience or things go quiet, it often indicates that people are engaged by what you are saying or are paying careful consideration to the question you've posed or the statement you've made. Silence can be a good thing, as it allows your audience with time to think, so take a slow, deep breath in between and calm yourself down. This is your breathing space, but it also makes an impact on your audience.

- Stay focused on the speech, rather than solely on the audience – while it's important to pay some attention to your audience, remember to focus on the task at hand. Focus on your material, your notes, your presentation, and your delivery. If you stay calm and focus on the messages you're sending, your audience may not even realize that you're nervous.

There is support out there if you find that you struggle with public speaking, so don't be afraid to attend training sessions, visit a coach, or attend groups and sessions with others who suffer speaking anxiety. Cognitive behavioral therapy can help you manage your negative thinking patterns when it comes to speaking too, so often, these strategies can help alleviate your symptoms and overcome your fear.

Right before you speak, you should visualize your success and do some deep breathing as we mentioned in Section 1 of this book. Calming your mind before you speak can really help you settle down before your gig, and even doing a few yoga stretches can help prepare you too.

Speaking is difficult if your self-esteem is low, and so many people feel they are not worthy enough of sharing their stories or expertise, which often results in anxiety-related symptoms. Combatting this in the long-term is a journey, so it takes time; there's no instant fix.

One thing we don't do enough is celebrate our own successes. This is something you need to get used to, especially when you're trying to overcome speaking anxieties and low-self-esteem. Doing this can encourage you in the future, make you feel good, boost your motivation, and generally, help you make the switch from negative to positive thinking. While celebrating your success can feel uncomfortable at first, you will get used to it, so keep at it.

*After your speech or presentation (or anything else you do that has caused you anxiety), congratulate yourself. Pat yourself on the back and share your success with others. Of course, your speech may not have been perfect, but this is an opportunity for you to learn. It's likely that you are your biggest critic, so make a list of development points so that the next time you deliver a speech, you can adjust and make those improvements. It's all a learning curve!

Anxiety symptoms and nerves are common in certain situations, especially when you're speaking in public. If you have social anxiety, this could amplify your speaking anxiety, so there could be other things that increase your level of fear. If you are struggling to overcome your speaking anxiety, speak to your doctor. They may be able to recommend a therapist, prescribe some calming medication, or even provide you with useful advice that will all help to reduce your fear whilst getting to the root cause.

Remember, public speaking is a skill that you have the power to improve; you can do it.

> "People will forget what you said, people will forget what you did, but people will never forget how you made them feel."
>
> ~ Maya Angelou

Now we've got to grips with public speaking, we're going to get a bit more general because there are so many different types of anxiety. We're going to talk about facing the most common anxieties in everyday life...

Chapter 14

Facing Anxiety from Everyday Life

In this chapter, we're going to explore the different types of everyday anxiety symptoms that many people experience. There are so many things that we encounter on a daily basis that can increase our anxiety levels, which means it's impossible to avoid completely.

In this section, we're going to talk about the different problems you can encounter that can trigger your anxiety, how you can be more prepared for the inevitable triggers, and as a result, gain more control over how you react in response to those triggers. We'll also explore the importance of overcoming everyday anxiety by discussing what can happen if you don't.

It's time to disentangle your anxiety and live your best life, regardless of the symptoms you encounter.

What Kind of Anxiety Comes in Everyday Life?

Anxiety symptoms are something we can't always avoid or prevent. While there are many different things that cause us stress throughout our lives, sometimes we encounter the inevitable or unexpected, and our anxiety is triggered as a result.

Everyday anxiety can be caused by:

- Financial issues
- Our children
- A death in the family
- A heavy workload
- Issues or repairs in the home
- Car repairs
- Health issues
- Skipping meals
- Medications
- Caffeine
- Negative thinking
- Conflict
- Social or public events

There's nothing we can do about it when these things happen. While we can't control the things that happen, we can control the way we respond if they do. The best thing to do is be prepared in advance for such things.

Being prepared doesn't mean you sit and worry in case something happens. It simply means you don't have to worry because you have a plan of action in case the inevitable occurs. You don't have to fully commit to expecting such an event, but you should have a little plan in place ahead of time.

Facing Anxiety from Everyday Life

*Take out your journal and write down some everyday anxieties that you believe you'll encounter at some point in your life. Note down what you can do if this occurs. For example, if you have health issues, make a plan to fully engage with your doctor, educate yourself on the illness, and respond proactively. Or if you find yourself having financial issues, maybe you'll make arrangements to speak to a financial advisor and be more careful with your money. With many of the problems that occur in life, it's a good idea to make a plan to save up an emergency fund in case it's needed as being a little more financially secure can improve your anxiety symptoms. Even saving up some of your vacation days at work can mean that if some kind of emergency occurs, you don't need to worry about taking unpaid time off.

In addition, you need to be able to prioritize things in your life effectively, so that if you become overwhelmed, you can focus on the most important things. This prevents you from having larger obligations if a crisis arises.

This book has concentrated on remaining positive because it's an important part of overcoming your anxiety, however, when your anxiety symptoms are managed well, there's no reason why you can't be prepared for some events that are beyond your control. That's because these things may trigger your anxiety if you don't have a proactive plan in place, so you won't feel as anxious. Of course, we can't promise it will completely take away every symptom as there are things that cause our anxiety levels to increase, but having some kind of contingency provides us with some comfort and direction.

Why is This Form of Anxiety Important to Overcome?

If you don't deal with your everyday anxieties, they can pile up and fester. This leads to further issues, for example, you could become depressed as the anxiety builds, or you could even develop bad habits as a result of it.

To prevent this from happening, you must deal with your anxieties and learn to overcome them. We've talked so much already about handling your anxieties, so you have the skills to deal with your everyday anxieties already, you simply have to put those things into practice by learning how unexpected anxiety triggers affect you.

If you don't overcome your everyday anxieties, you'll start to feel like you're in an endless loop of exhaustion. Rather than getting over your anxiety, you'll make it worse and before you know it, you'd have fallen into a downward spiral of anxiety which can mean your health deteriorates.

Anxiety should never be ignored, and there are ways to prepare in advance for those unexpected anxious moments.

How Can I Be Prepared for Anxious Moments in My Life?

We have covered so much already in this book, so you're more prepared for those anxious moments than you think. Let's quickly explore some of the top tips to help you prevent or manage the anxieties of life you may encounter.

If you have financial worries, talking to someone you trust about this means you're sharing the load, which can make a huge difference in your life. You should respond in a proactive way, going through all your incomings and outgoings, and seeking financial advice if necessary.

If you're worried about a health condition, you need to assess your situation. We're always going to worry if we have a health condition, but there are things we can do to reduce the level of worry. For example, if you keep your body as fit and healthy as possible, and ensure you eat the right foods, your general health is likely to be better. If you do have a health condition, make sure you do all you can to maintain your health, and make any lifestyle changes you need to make. Be open to your doctor's advice and be open and honest with your family.

Grief is something that can cause severe anxiety too, but death is part of life's natural cycle, so it's something that we all experience. You must accept that death happens, and it's something that we can't control. As it's so final, it often makes us feel insecure or unsafe, and while you shouldn't sit around worrying about losing loved ones, you shouldn't avoid the topic of death and there's no harm in having a plan. It's natural for you to feel scared in case you lose somebody else or even think about how much time you have left. The situation is stressful because we don't really understand it, and losing someone is a traumatic experience. Being able to accept death is a key way of getting through this time, and keeping yourself in good physical and mental health, increases your ability to cope. Exercising, meditation, changing your habits and receiving professional help can all help you in overcoming your anxieties around death after it's happened, so if you believe that death will impact you dramatically, find a few good therapists that specializes in dealing with bereavement and ensure you keep their details in a safe place so you can contact them if you need to.

If you have a hectic job with an endless workload, you may find that your workload is causing you stress and anxiety. You can plan for this by ensuring you have time to unwind and destress when you're home from work, and you could also talk to your boss about this. If you feel particularly stressed at work in the middle of your shift, you could schedule in five minutes to practice deep breathing techniques. Guided meditations at the beginning of the day can help with focus and productivity, while those in the evening can help you relax and improve your sleep.

We often encounter conflict in our day-to-day life, and it can be difficult to stay calm when they occur unexpectedly, especially if this is something we feel passionate about. While you can't always avoid or control conflict, you can consider what you'll do if you encounter conflict. You should:

- Accept that conflict happens – it's natural!
- Remain calm – even if the other person is being aggressive or saying irrational things, you should stay calm but firm.
- Listen to the other person – it's important that you listen to the person that you have the conflict with and engage with them.
- Empathize with the other person – you need to show you understand their side of the story, but calmly explain your side too.

- Take your time and think before you respond – sometimes we react too quickly without thinking. Make sure you take your time, so you use up some valuable thinking time before you respond.
- Accept responsibility – if you have some responsibility in this, always accept this on your part.
- Look for common ground – if you can find something in common with the person you have conflict with, it's often easier to work together and find a solution.
- Try to find a solution, or if not, agree to disagree – we don't have to agree on everything!
- Move on and focus on the future – once the conflict is over, you need to move on in a positive way. Whatever your differences, it's important to wipe the slate clean and concentrate on the future.

Many different things cause us stress and anxiety. For instance, we could need repairs to our home or car, but if we have a little money saved, and insurances, we can save ourselves the anxiety of wondering how we can pay for those repairs if we already have a plan. Keeping the contact details of good repairmen is also a way to alleviate your anxiety when the unexpected occurs, because you know exactly who to contact regarding your situation.

You have so much knowledge of anxiety now, so when it occurs unexpectedly, it's likely that you recognize the signs but if you're unsure what to do next, simply head back to Section 1 and work your way through chapters 3-5 and follow the steps most appropriate to your anxious situation. These are the steps you can continue to use as and when required, whenever an anxious situation crosses your path.

You're not alone in your anxiety, but you have the tools required to disentangle your symptoms. It's time you see this and embrace your new-found knowledge and skills.

You've got this!

Conclusion

Conclusion

Chapter 15

It's Not About Control; It's About Commitment

This is just a small chapter because it's important to have breathing space to allow you to pause and think. It's also important to celebrate how far you've come. You've certainly shown commitment and determination so far.

As we move into the final section of this book, it's time to keep the momentum going when it comes to your anxiety. So, let's talk about what your anxiety symptoms are or are not.

Combating your symptoms of anxiety in the long term is not a simple task, it's a life-long journey and it does mean change. Let me explain...

> *"Just when the caterpillar thought the world was ending, he turned into a butterfly."*
>
> ~ *Anonymous proverb*

Perception is everything. The caterpillar's metamorphosis is a symbol of hope and shows you that when you believe things are as bad as they can get, you still have the power to make your transformation into something as mesmerizing as a butterfly. Not only is a butterfly beautiful, but it also leaves its cocoon with the knowledge of how to fly, which means after being caged, it's finally free. Of course, it faces new challenges but it's reborn into something new. There's no reason why you can't be reborn too!

The butterfly starts out as a slow caterpillar that munches its way through life. It's pretty slow-moving and is soon caged in its own cocoon. Life seems pretty uneventful and maybe even boring.

At the beginning of this book, you were the caterpillar. Your anxiety symptoms were your cocoon and you realized what was happening, you were tangled in it. You were trapped. You probably felt safe in your cocoon, but you couldn't stay there forever. That's because anxiety is a journey, just as life is.

In fact, anxiety is not just a journey, it's a commitment. The biggest you'll ever face!

It's not the intention of this book to spook you by telling you that anxiety is the biggest commitment you'll ever face, but it's important you know the truth. It's not a commitment you need to shy away from, because you already have the tools you need to disentangle it and keep it at bay, but the symptoms are not exactly something that should be or need to be controlled; however, they are something we need to be able to recognize and cope with if necessary.

Let's use the caterpillar versus the butterfly analogy to explain a little more...

It's Not About Control; It's About Commitment

The caterpillar is committed to eating its way through leaves to give its body what it needs, and then patiently awaits its transformation to occur. It doesn't know what to expect, but it follows its path.

You started this book figuring out what anxiety is, and what signs and symptoms you present. You considered the severity of your symptoms and thought about whether or not you have anxiety, while also learning self-acceptance and how to identify your own anxiety symptoms. You worked on the guidance and tools provided in this book and researched more about your anxiety, and your triggers, and put in place a plan of attack because you're committed to disentangling your anxiety symptoms and building a stronger understanding of it.

Since then, you've learned to listen to yourself, and you know how to take care of your mind, body, and spirit, the importance of taking time for yourself, how to plan effectively to ensure you are more organized and build self-care into your life, as well as everything else you have to do, and you've done this well. You understand that perspective is everything, and you've even worked on altering your own perspective to ensure you have a more positive outlook.

You've never wavered with your commitment, as still, you've focused on different types of anxiety and how you can face them. This includes facing your fear of responsibility, relationship anxiety, speaking anxiety, along with other common general anxieties in everyday life.

Your commitment has taken you this far, and you're making your transformation, but there are some things you need to consider as we head into the final part of your journey before you're fully transformed and ready for your new, exciting life...

That's why, in this chapter, we're going to talk about committing to your life as we disentangle your anxiety.

You're Doing Great!

It's important to know that if you're already identifying the causes of your anxiety, managing your anxiety, and overcoming the anxieties in aspects of your life, you can deal with anything.

You're doing great!

There's one important fact that we need to discuss here, as while it's important to keep your anxiety symptoms under control, you must recognize that managing your anxiety does not mean controlling every aspect of your life. Sometimes, the unexpected occurs and this is not necessarily a bad thing. It can be a good thing too.

You shouldn't aim to 'control' everything, but you should commit to:

- Embracing a positive mindset
- Taking action against your anxieties
- Overcoming the barriers that stand in your way

While you can't prevent everything, you can reduce the level of anxiety you feel by practicing the things you've learned so far. While the learning chapters of this book are now over, you're about to face the biggest obstacle you've had to face so far on your journey, before you break from your cocoon.

It's Not About Control; It's About Commitment

You've got a hard hill to climb, but this section is the final hurdle. You have all the tools, skills, and knowledge you need to succeed, so all you have to do is commit. This book has never claimed that anxiety is easy, nor has it claimed that it can diagnose or cure your anxiety, but you know that already as only a medical professional can do this. When a person experiences symptoms of anxiety, they know how difficult it can be to identify and overcome it because something inside wants them to submit, give in, or back down, but they're here because they're fighters. You're doing something about your anxiety because you're not willing to allow it to place limitations on your life anymore.

You're already rising to the challenges you've faced but staying on the route can be difficult because there are always bumps in the road that will try to hinder your progress or even send you in the wrong direction. Beating anxiety means constantly getting back on track whenever something stands in your way. This could be prior or post-transformation, as there's no use sugar-coating it, disentangling your anxiety is a lifelong journey and it's tough, but over time, it does become a habit.

In the chapters to follow, we're going to clarify some important points regarding anxiety and its symptoms, because we want you to succeed in your goal to overcome it, and in order to do this, we need to make sure you're fully informed.

Your first top tip is to make sure that you are not viewing anxiety as something that can be controlled, trapped, and stored away. If you want to disentangle your anxiety and increase your understanding of this, you need to recognize that it's part of life, but sometimes you may need to intervene in order to cope or remedy its symptoms if need be. You don't have to allow your symptoms to take over your life, but only you can stop them.

In the next chapter, we'll talk about anxiety and how it can lead to deception. This is certainly something you're going to want to know.

Chapter 16

Anxiety Can Lead to Deception

Whilst some anxiety is good (we'll cover this in the next chapter), other anxiety symptoms can be negative and try to deceive you.

We've got something extremely important to share with you...

> If anxiety is trying to deceive you, it is NOT your friend!

This book is here to give you information and provide you with the guidance you need because we've been there when it comes to anxiety. Your anxiety symptoms make you believe untrue things that impact you or others; it's a deceiver. It will continue to deceive you for as long as you let it. It doesn't want to be vanquished or regulated, it wants to control you, but you're not going to let it, because you're leading through anxiety and you're ready for anything.

In this chapter, we're going to consider three common questions asked by a person who is being deceived by their anxiety. We're going to discuss what you can do if you fall into bad habits, or if you don't think you're good enough. We're also going to talk through combatting your anxiety, even if you don't have a goal to aim for, as we want to ensure that nothing stands in your way as you make your transformation and break free from your cocoon.

There's no time to waste because anxiety has wasted so much of your time already, so let's get to it...

What if I Fall Into Bad Habits?

The anxiety that is trying to deceive you, wants you to believe that:

- You can't change
- You will fall back into bad habits
- There's no coming back from your bad habits, as they'll keep taking over

Let's say you've worked to identify the root causes and triggers of your anxiety symptoms, you've got a plan of action and things are going really well, but then, suddenly, you slip back into bad habits...

That little voice in your head that's controlled by your anxiety and its symptoms wants you to give up and revert back to your anxious ways, but you've come too far for that now. You know exactly how to deal with those bad habits. You're better than this and you know it!

The first thing you should do if you find you're slipping back into bad habits is take a step back and accept that we all have a blip from time to time; this is just a setback. It's not a failure; your anxiety has not won.

You should then list down the bad habits you've got. Maybe you're not exercising, or you're indulging in too much screen time. Both of these things can set off your anxiety over time, so, as soon as you recognize you are doing this, make a note of it.

Take some time to really consider what's triggering your bad habit, and reflect. Try some deep breathing or meditation techniques and ask yourself: *When can I recall doing this for the first time? How does it make me feel? What are the benefits of changing this habit?* You really need this to be clear in your mind, but if you want to prevent this from happening in the future, you need to be aware of what's causing you to slip.

You already have the tools you need to start replacing your bad habits with new, positive habits that are of benefit to you, so once you know what bad habits you want to change, create or adjust your plan of action.

You really have got this! Making a change is that simple and although it does require commitment from you, the concept itself is not difficult. Sometimes, we have blips because we begin to neglect ourselves again, so a bit of self-care can go a long way. Most of all, forgive. Don't be hard on yourself. You've spotted the bad habit and you're working on ways to overcome this, so celebrate your progress. Awareness is always the first step, and by recognizing this, you've already shown that you've started reprogramming your thought patterns.

What if I Don't Think I'm Good Enough?

Of course, your anxiety wants you to believe you're not good enough. The fact is, anxiety despises confidence because if you have confidence, your anxiety symptoms will be minimal.

You are good enough, and you need to remember how valuable you are. You have to stop anxiety from beating back your confidence because it's time to switch it up… It's time for your confidence to beat back your anxiety by disentangling it.

We all suffer from feelings of self-doubt from time to time, so you're not alone if you believe you're not good enough. It's worth knowing that if you are feeling like this, it's most likely that there's an underlying issue you need to explore as this often leads to self-sabotage.

If you start to feel like you're not good enough, you should:

- Talk to someone you trust about how you feel.
- Limit the time you spend with negative people.
- Start building your confidence by:
  - Tracking your progress
  - Make a list of the things you're good at
  - Learn or refine a new skill
  - Ask your friends what you're good at
  - Celebrate your wins and successes every day
- Stop comparing yourself to others, and set your own personal goals based on what you want to achieve.
- Take care of your mind by exercising, eating healthily, and meditating.

What if I Don't Have a Purpose to Aim for?

Your anxiety symptoms can make it difficult for you to find a purpose to aim for, in fact, you may start to believe you don't even have one. Let me assure you, you do have a purpose. You just haven't figured it out yet. Many people find it easy to discover their purpose, but for some, it's much more challenging. It's not always easy to focus on one key thing or figure out what to aim for.

Anxiety clouds our judgment and sometimes we can't see past it. Just concentrating on the present is important as it can help us get our anxiety symptoms under control. As we're facing our struggles, it's really difficult to focus on what we want for the future. We don't always believe it's positive and therefore, we don't want to focus on a glum future.

"You don't have to control your thoughts. You just have to stop letting them control you."

~ Dan Millman

Even if the future is difficult to think about right now, we all have hopes, aspirations and dreams, so you will be able to figure out your purpose, it could just take some time. Just relax, and don't stress it. Take some time to work on you first and focus on self-care. Work on ways to clear your mind and refocus, by keeping up with your exercise regime, following your schedule, meditating, eating healthily, and taking some time to kick back and reflect. Once you start to calm your mind again, you can start to work on your purpose but remember, you don't have to know this instantly. It's okay to change your purpose as your vision changes.

When figuring out your purpose, you must explore your strengths and talents. Really consider the things you're good at and consider what you'd like to use your strengths for. You should also consider your aspirations and consider where you want to be in the next 5-10 years.

Don't be afraid to use visualization techniques; visualize how you want things to look in the future.

If you're still not sure, you should think about:

- What are you working towards?
- What direction do my actions send me in?
- What are you passionate about?

Start small, and figure out your short-term purpose, and consider the things you want to achieve over the next 6-12 months. Maybe you want to improve your anxiety, develop your career, or even lose weight and enhance your general health. When your judgment becomes less clouded and you're ready to embrace the future, follow the steps below:

1. Create a personal vision statement that reflects your desires and aspirations
2. Write lists of:
    a. The things you love to do
    b. What you're good at
    c. Your strengths
    d. Your talents

Anxiety Can Lead to Deception

    e. Your hopes and dreams
    f. Your beliefs and morals
    g. Your aspirations

3. Figure out your values – what's important to you (ALWAYS) as you journey through life?
4. Practice celebrating your wins
5. Journal daily, and check in with yourself on a weekly basis – *are you still heading towards your goals? Have your goals changed in anyway? Do they align with your purpose?*
6. Acknowledge the things you don't like – accept them and consider how you can take action to change things.
7. Take time to reflect by practicing breathing exercises, thinking time, mindfulness, and meditation.

Your purpose is your why and even if you're not entirely sure of this yet, you'll figure out your purpose by listening to yourself, tuning into your intuition, and observing your actions, because actions speak louder than words.

Symptoms of anxiety are something you must continue to defeat along your journey, before it swallows you up in its deception. If you have a purpose, it's a threat to anxiety, so if it's been controlling you for some time, it will be trying to push you into believing you don't have or need a purpose. You're not being told this to instill fear, it's simply warning you of the impacts of anxiety that you're going to want to avoid, because they can set you back.

Remember, awareness is everything!

Chapter 17

Anxiety isn't Always a Bad Thing!

You know so much about disentangling your anxiety already, but it's time to get even wiser about it. While we've talked about anxiety deceiving you, you need to remember that not all anxiety is bad. We've spoken about bad and good anxiety already in the early stages of this book, but it's important to clarify this in more detail.

It's your time, and it's down to you to recognize the signs and tune into your anxiety so you can identify the good from the bad. In this chapter, we're going to recap the meaning of anxiety and consider why it's important to recognize good anxiety.

Finally, you'll be presented with some useful tips to help you change your point of view when it comes to anxiety and begin to look at this in a new light.

> *"When you change the way you look at things, the things you look at change."*
>
> *~ Wayne Dyer*

Let's get down to business by clarifying what anxiety means to you. You may find your whole perspective changes, because there are many people who use anxiety in a positive way.

What Does Anxiety Mean to You?

There's no use sugar-coating it, anxiety and its symptoms are often seen as awful things. Most of us want to run away from them, but this is only one perspective on anxiety. We should never run from anxiety. Let me explain...

Anxiety is emotional; it can include feeling scared, worried, or tense about something that could happen soon. For some of us, it makes us feel threatened, and stirs up a range of feelings, physical sensations, and thoughts. This causes our senses to heighten, and we feel on edge.

Feelings of anxiety are normal. It's a natural human response that can be useful to us, and we'll talk about this soon, but before we do, it's important to know that anxiety only usually becomes problematic when it becomes a mental health problem, and when this happens, you need to see your doctor.

Anxiety becomes a mental health problem if it impacts or impairs your ability to function and prevents you from living your life as you want to. If you find yourself blowing your worries and fears out of proportion, avoiding certain situations in your life, or struggling to control your feelings of distress, then your anxiety could be spiraling, and becoming a mental health problem.

You are already aware of the signs and symptoms that suggest anxiety is a problem, but as we've mentioned already, not all anxiety is bad. We know about the bad, so now, let's talk about good anxiety.

Most people feel anxiety because they care about something, and caring is a positive thing. It's good to care about things! While the feelings that show as a result of feeling anxiety are not pleasant, it can help us make sound judgments in difficult or emergency situations. For example, it helps us to sense danger, or if someone suffered an injury and we want to help them, it can motivate us to respond appropriately.

When you manage your anxiety well, you'll be able to differentiate between good and bad anxiety. You'll be able to tap into your 'good' anxiety and use it to inspire, drive, or motivate. Confidence can be a big part of this as it shows you're doing your best as you actually care about the outcome.

Why is it Important to See Anxiety as a Good Thing?

While there is a negative spin attached to anxiety, it can be used for the greater good. When anxiety is managed and is not spiraling out of control, it's actually a good way to:

- Protect yourself – your anxiety can act as a warning if you're in danger and always aims to protect you. Let's say it's late and you're walking down a dark street, it alerts you that there's a possibility of danger.

- Motivate yourself – your anxiety can spur you into taking action, so it can give you the kick up the bum you need to move forward.

- Ensure you make decisions fast – if you need to think on your feet and make a quick decision, anxiety can help you to quickly way up the pros and cons, and make a faster decision.

- Trust your intuition – when you're anxious all of the time, it can be difficult to trust how you feel because your anxiety is not under control, which means it's not rational. When it is, your anxiety can provide you with signs suggesting if something is a good or bad idea. You can learn to use these signs when tuning into your intuition as your anxiety can aid that.

- Improve your self-confidence – when your anxiety is at a manageable level and you're making good decisions in your life, your self-confidence improves. This is because you're not only taking care of yourself, but you're also learning to trust yourself too.

There are many arguments regarding the positive side of anxiety. Many people believe that if you're an anxious person, you're highly intelligent, and develop strong research, critical thinking, and analyzing skills. It's also believed you are able to understand and process information easily, and it also highlights what's important to you, including your deep core values.

If you can work out what's causing your symptoms of anxiety, you can use it as a motivation to get things done, and your anxiety will help by pushing you into taking action and as a result, it can help you reach your full potential.

As with everything in life, we need balance and a certain amount of anxiety in your life is normal in some situations. You're never going to delete it from your life completely and you shouldn't want to.

It's time to start looking at anxiety in a different way!

How Can I Begin to Look at Anxiety in a New Light?

Changing what you believe about anxiety isn't a quick fix, as it takes place over a period of time. First, let's draw your attention to a very important fact regarding anxiety...

*Experts believe that most people have a negative bias when it comes to anxiety and therefore, they are more likely to pay attention as it's seen as being scary or threatening.

While the aim of this section is to get you thinking more positively about anxiety, it's important to acknowledge that there is already a negative connotation attached to anxiety. By seeing it differently, and by practicing optimism, you can change how you feel about anxiety, and look at this in a more positive way.

But how can you become more optimistic?

The most important thing when you are practicing optimism is that you need to be realistic. If you're not, you won't truly believe in it, and therefore, you'll continue to dwell on the negatives. Optimism can reduce negative feelings associated with anxiety and can make you feel more positive in everything you do.

Here are some top tips to help you become more optimistic:

1. Retrain your brain to think differently – identify your negative thought patterns through your journalling, and challenge them; *Why are you thinking like that? Is there any evidence to suggest this?* You should then replace your thinking with positive statements. So, if you think 'I can't do that' replace this with 'I can do that.' This takes time, as you must use repetition to reprogram how you handle your negative thoughts and respond. Obviously, the key is to start recognizing the negative thoughts first, so you can switch them into optimistic statements.

2. Every morning, when you wake, set a positive intention – start writing down a goal for the day or something that you want to do that's positive. This will help you embrace a positive mindset and if you want to go one step further, keep a gratitude journal, so you can note down all the things you're grateful for.

3. Dismantle your fears – there's always a cause behind your fear, and in order to get over your fear, you must unpick it first so you can recognize the reason behind it. When you start to feel anxious, consider why you're feeling this way? Then consider what's the worst that can happen and what's the likelihood of it happening? We often blow things out of proportion, so it's important to put things into perspective. Consider the likelihood of this being resolved or changed? Also, how will it impact your life? What else contributed to this event? Are there any underlying factors? Next, think about how you can change the outcome: what do you want to happen instead? You can then put steps in place to ensure things happen in a more positive way. This will help you build your self-confidence too.

4. Make a list of people who make you feel good and make a conscious effort to spend time with them. Having positive social relationships ensures you feel calm and safe, and their positivity will spread as it's infectious! You just have to let it in.

5. Embrace optimism by surrounding yourself in it – this doesn't mean just spending time with other optimistic people, try attending positive training sessions or community groups that are filled with people who want to help others and give back to the community. You should also practice gratitude, be mindful and remind yourself of the things you're looking forward to, but most of all, be kind to yourself. Leave yourself positive notes and celebrate your successes too, don't be afraid to share these!

6. Smile more – while many people believe that if you smile, you need something to smile for, but smiling can also make you feel happy and joyful too. Making a conscious effort to smile more actually reduces anxiety and it has a psychological impact on your mindset. Many people who make a conscious effort smile actually start to feel happier and have a more positive outlook.

7. Try 15 minutes of yoga every morning – yoga is a great way to relax and calm your mind but stretching your body and concentrating on your breathing can prepare you well for the day ahead too. Fifteen minutes each day can make a huge impact on your life, for the better.

Of course, some anxiety is unjustified and unnecessary, but you have the skills to take a step back and assess whether your anxiety is, or is not, reasonable. If we care about something, that's a positive thing so you should smile. Your anxiety is occurring for a valid reason, which means it's justified. If you're challenging how you feel, you're doing the right thing and responding how you should. This is all part of disentangling your anxiety.

In the next chapter, we're going to talk about where you can find some relief from your anxiety symptoms if you find that you're struggling. Anxiety wants you to feel like you're alone as you battle against it, but that's just not true...

If you don't know this already, you should!

While there's a stigma attached to anxiety, it's worth remembering that while you're focused on being more optimistic, you're challenging this stigma and challenging the deception that anxiety causes. This means you're a change-maker and that's awesome, you're ready for the battle ahead!

Chapter 18

Where to Find Relief

The reason anxiety is so powerful is that it creeps up on you and slowly grinds you down. Sometimes you don't even notice it. We all need a break or some kind of relief from its grasp from time to time, so in this chapter, we're going to ensure you're ready to continue disentangling your anxiety beyond this book by ensuring you know what to do when your anxiety is becoming a little too much and you need some relief.

"People become attached to their burdens sometimes more than the burdens are attached to them."

~ George Bernard Shaw

Sometimes, we choose not to share how we feel and we choose not to share our burdens. *Guess what?* Anxiety doesn't want you to share these things. It wants you to bottle them up so that it gains power... But you're not going to let this happen.

Knowing when to detach yourself from the burdens of anxiety is important, and Shaw is right in the quote above when he says you are more attached to your burdens than they are to you.

So, just let them go...

Remember the self-acceptance chapter in Section 1 of this book (Chapter 3 to be precise)? While it's important to accept yourself and accept anxiety, it's just as important to accept when you need relief from your symptoms too. When you're combatting each day, you may need to relieve some of the symptoms so you can increase your energy levels and take a step back to refocus. That's why this chapter will be exploring what others can do to help with your anxiety, and why it's so important to have the support of others. We'll also be considering how others can make a difference in your life while removing some of the anxiety symptoms you feel.

Let's lead through the anxiety together so you can lead a life free from the restraints of anxiety. Before we lead into the first section of this chapter, pay attention to the quote below:

"Calm mind brings inner strength and self-confidence, so that's very important for good health."

~ Dalai Lama

Your anxiety isn't serving you, so stop feeding it!

What Can Others Do to Help with Anxiety?

There are many ways that others can help and support you when your anxiety symptoms are troubling you. There are also a lot of people who can help you with your

Where to Find Relief

anxiety symptoms—more than you probably realize—as anxiety is much more recognized now, being a common problem that impacts so many people. There is much more awareness about the impact anxiety can have on a person's life and that's a good thing, as catching it early or having prevention methods is key to beating back anxiety.

People who could help you with your anxiety could include close family and friends whom you trust, doctors, therapists or counselors, support groups, and psychotherapists or psychiatrists. Let's talk about how each of these groups of people can support you:

- Friends and family whom you trust – if you explain to close family or friends how you feel, they'll be willing to support you because they care about you. To support you, they can simply listen to you, exercise with you, help you practice breathing exercises, or even help you put your anxieties into perspective. They can also:
  - Offer to accompany you to any appointments you have
  - Arrange a doctor's appointment for you
  - Research different support options available in your area
  - Help you find a therapist

Just having someone to turn to can make a huge difference!

- Doctors – if you feel that your anxiety is taking over, and you're suffering from numerous symptoms, it's worth speaking to your doctor as they may be able to signpost you to others or treat you themselves. Occasionally, they prescribe medication if need be.

- Therapists or counselors – if you're having trouble with your anxiety, a counselor or therapist can help you with that and they can treat you with a range of therapies, including holistic therapies to help you relax, CBT or DBT (or other relevant talking therapies), and they may even offer hypnosis and meditation to help you overcome your anxiety.

- Support groups – there are many anxiety support groups out there that can help you come to terms with your anxiety. This gives you the opportunity to listen to others and their journey with anxiety, as well as talking through your own anxiety. Remember, anxiety wants you to think you're alone, but if you attend a support group, you'll realize this isn't the case. They can suggest and share coping techniques, as well as provide you with a safe space to disclose how you feel.

- Psychotherapists and psychiatrists – they specialize in mental health, so if your anxiety has become a mental health issue, they can assess you and put together a plan of action to help you overcome your anxiety and they'll check in on you by keeping in communication and monitoring your progress.

The wisdom provided in this book so far works well against anxiety symptoms, and by now, you even recognize that anxiety is not always a bad thing. There are times when you need people in your corner, but it really is amazing how much support is out there, so make a promise to yourself right now...

Promise that you WILL ask for support from others if you need to, as you need those cheerleaders on your side. This is vital!

You've read all the advice and tips we've provided in this book so far, and we won't let you down. But you also know that anxiety wants you to feel alone, and you've heard the warning of what anxiety can do if you do not overcome it… That's loud and clear, so it's now time to do something about it!

Why is it Important to Have the Support of Others?

As we've said repeatedly, your anxiety wants you to feel alone. There are many people out there who can help to support you when you have anxiety issues, you just have to figure out who is part of your support network.

Your support network refers to the people in your life that help you achieve your goals. When it comes to your anxiety, having a support network can make a huge difference as it can speed up your recovery time, and also provide you with the reassurance that if you slide into bad anxiety-related habits, you have people you can turn to, to help you out or give you a kick up the butt.

Having a good support network can really have a positive impact on your life. If you have:

1. Great friends
2. An experienced mentor
3. A qualified therapist
4. Good support groups

You'll find your anxiety symptoms improve because it allows you to talk about and work through your triggers. They will encourage you to keep striving toward your goals and disentangle your anxiety.

Your support network will ultimately keep you on the right track and ensure you remain motivated throughout the more difficult times, so you have the power to completely crush the anxiety symptoms you're facing. Having people to turn to in your hour of need helps you get back on track quickly, and prevents you from stewing, before escalating the situation.

If you find that you're struggling to get back on your feet, you can go back to the people in your support network as they will give you a helping hand, so you can pick yourself up. They'll also be honest with you, so if you're starting to let your anxiety spiral, they'll let you know.

While your network is there to provide you with the support you need, it's important that it's a positive experience. Not everything related to anxiety MUST be negative as that would be counterproductive.

With that in mind, there's one extremely important thing you need to do, also...

You must also go to your support network when things go right—celebrate your wins when you succeed. Trust me, they'll want to share this experience with you because they care about you and are very much invested in your success, just as much as you are.

When you're disentangling anxiety, you don't have to do it alone. Your support network can help you grow. Let's talk more about this.

How Can Others Make a Difference in My Growth?

Other people can make a huge difference to your development and growth, when you're working through or disentangling anxiety. With the right support, you'll feel motivated to overcome your fears and reach for those successes. They're already within your grasp.

Others can help you grow when you're suffering with your anxiety because:

- They can share their own knowledge and experience with you regarding anxiety, so you can learn something.

- They provide you with connection and as human beings, being socially connected to others improves our mental health.

- They give you comfort, and just knowing that they're there to support you can fill you with a little more confidence.

- It reminds you to be grateful. You have a good support network and you're not alone while battling your symptoms, which means you have something to be thankful for. Being thankful promotes a more positive atmosphere, overall.

- When you develop new connections and build positive relationships, it helps you improve the other relationships in your life too.

- Self-esteem and self-confidence contribute toward feelings of anxiety, so when others help and support you, and you feel grateful and generally more positive, you start to recognize your self-worth. Others help you see this clearly, which ultimately boosts your self-esteem and confidence. More confidence often leads to more success.

- Your support network will hold you accountable and keep you on the right track. It's difficult to stay motivated when you're going it alone, but if you have others who are checking on your progress, investing their time, and have your best interests at heart, you're more likely to want to succeed and achieve your goals, so therefore put more effort in. You'll find you don't only want to succeed for yourself, you also want to succeed for your support network too, so you can all celebrate together.

Finding relief for your anxiety symptoms is important, as you should have support when you need it. Having the support of others can make your recovery so much easier, because it's the time you finally realize who is on your side and who wants you to succeed.

Knowing you have others who support you is the final hurdle in overcoming your anxiety. While it will never disappear entirely, you're capable of sorting the bad from the good, and you are equipped to use your anxiety in the most effective way.

> *"Grant me the serenity to accept the things I cannot change, the courage to change the things I can, and the wisdom to know the difference."*
>
> *~ Reinhold Niebuhr*

In life, especially when we're dealing with anxious thoughts, we have to embrace acceptance and change, but on your anxiety journey so far, you've learned so much too. All that we have to do now, is consider what it will be like to live anxiety-free!

You're about to find out!

Chapter 19

Anxiety-Free Living

What's it like to lead an anxiety-free life? Doing so is certainly the next phase of your journey as you've finally overcome your anxiety and beat back the symptoms you've suffered along the way.

Imagine...

You wake up after the most restful sleep EVER. It's 6 AM and you feel great. You put on a pot of coffee and drink a glass of water, before doing 10 minutes of meditation and 15 minutes of yoga. After a quick shower, you're ready to face breakfast and sink the coffee—the aroma is circulating through the house, and it smells great!

You open your journal and write down three things you're grateful for today and three things you want to achieve by the end of the day. You're focused and ready for the day ahead.

You finish getting dressed and get into your car to drive to work. Your happy and energetic playlist is on in the car, so you sing yourself to work. All the tasks you have to do today flow well, and you're extremely productive. You have time to chat to colleagues, and your boss, and at lunchtime, you take a stroll through the park, soaking in the views of trees, the birds picking scraps of food from the grassy areas, and you take a moment to watch the water in the lake as it flows, slowly, splashing ever-so-gently. You take in a breath and head back to the office for the afternoon, in which your meeting with a top client goes well and your boss pats you on the back before you leave for the day. All is well!

Your gym clothes are in the boot of your car, so before you head home for dinner, you take a high-intensity cardio class. When you get home, your partner has run your bath, so you can soak in the tub before you share your evening meal together. Together you share stories of your day and snuggle up on the couch for some TV time, talking over your plans for the weekend.

You head up to bed 30 minutes early and spend 15 minutes reading then 10 minutes journalling. You just have enough time for a quick 5-minute wind-down meditation before it's lights out, and you drift off to sleep.

Sounds like the perfect day, right?

While this may not sound like your perfect anxiety-free day, it's certainly a good example of mine. This just gives you an idea of what it could be like to live anxiety-free.

Let me clarify, when we talk about living anxiety-free, we are referring to 'bad' anxiety. As you know, you need a certain level of anxiety as it can help you make active and important decisions quickly. You already have the tools you need to assess your personal levels of anxiety and to also separate the bad examples of anxiety from the good, and it's now up to you to implement this.

You're more than capable of doing this!

Your Perfect Day

Now we know my idea of a perfect, anxiety-free day, you need to figure out yours. Just follow the steps below:

1. Take a deep breath in through the nose for 4 seconds. Hold for 4 seconds. Breathe out through the mouth for 5 seconds. Repeat 3 times.
2. Return to your natural breathing pattern and close your eyes.
3. Imagine your perfect anxiety-free day from waking up until you go to sleep, first in your head.
4. Wiggle your fingers and toes, and slowly bring yourself back into the present. When you're ready, open your eyes.
5. Write down (or draw) your experience—describing the details including the time you wake, what you do, and don't forget to use your senses—describe what you can see, smell, taste, touch, and hear. If you're drawing, make sure you're still appealing to the senses as you want this visualization of your perfect day to be as clear as possible.

This is what your perfect anxiety-free day looks like, and all you have to do now is create your goals: *What steps do you need to take for this visualization to become real?*

Be sure to set those goals, because your anxiety-free living is within your grasp. You've just got to reach out and grab it.

Your Progress With Anxiety

We're proud of you!

We're so pleased with the progress you've made so far when it comes to your anxiety and how you've got those symptoms under control. You've shown real grit and determination throughout your journey so far. While nobody ever lives entirely anxiety-free, you will experience anxiety-free days, and you deserve to enjoy them.

If you disentangle your anxiety by following and engaging with this book from start to finish, your anxiety symptoms will become less of a problem. Your visualization of a perfect day is just a snippet of what you can achieve if you follow the tips and advice provided.

You're a change-maker and you're changing both your lifestyle and mindset. It's time to invest and believe in yourself, because you've made so much progress already.

Look at your goals from the beginning of this book. You'll be making steady progress toward accomplishing these if you haven't already. You'll soon need to set some more goals to keep the momentum going.

You've had time to discover your new-found passions in life and we're eager to know what they are. When we're anxious, it takes the enjoyment out of life, but there will certainly be things in life that you've suddenly grown passionate about. A clear mind enjoys life so much more and embraces their passions, so...

*Grab a notebook or some paper and list the things you like or like to do. Anything new since you started working on your anxiety issues. *What gives you enjoyment? Is there* *anything you're doing or enjoying that you never thought possible?*

When we have overcome our anxiety issues, the things we always thought impossible often become possibility for us. This gives us hope because you've taken the opportunity to identify, understand, and overcome your anxiety symptoms, before they take over your life. Now, anything is possible. *The only question is, how high can you reach?*

You're on fire, so reach for the stars!

But... I'm Not Quite There Yet

If you're not quite there yet when it comes to your perfect, anxiety-free day, you shouldn't worry. Your visualization of your anxiety-free day is what you're aiming for; it's your aspiration.

But it's an aspiration within your grasp. You just have to keep striving towards this. It's the life you want, but your 'want' should be driving you to achieve it soon, rather than later.

It's all in your hands!

Your Future is in Your Hands

Your future is your own, and nobody can take that away from you. From this moment on, every decision you make regarding your anxiety is down to you; it always has been. If you want to truly overcome anxiety, you have to stay motivated and keep striving towards what you want, an anxiety-free life!

There really are no excuses you can make now. You have all the tools and tips you need to disentangle your anxiety, and all you have to do is apply what you've learned.

You know how to identify your anxiety triggers and accept who you are. You know how to deal with the symptoms of anxiety and formulate a plan of attack, while also taking care of your body and mind. You've explored different scenarios and put the final touches together so you can overcome it.

Now, it's decision time...

Will you make the decision to implement the tools you have?

Will you lead through anxiety using your tools and all the skills you've learned?

Will you implement the strategies that lead you to achieving your goals?

If you're saying *Yes. Yes. Yes.* You truly are ready to disentangle your anxiety.

The anxiety symptoms are yours and yours alone, so you must find ways to deal with it and use it to your advantage. If you truly want to live as anxiety-free as possible, you need to act.

> *"Every time you are tempted to react in the same old way, ask if you want to be a prisoner of the past or a pioneer of the future."*
>
> ~ Deepak Chopra

While you can't control everything in your life, you can have aspirations and goals, and you can work to accomplish those things. Changing your mindset, your thinking patterns, and your behaviors so you don't respond in the same way to the same problems can help you break the cycle of anxiety you constantly find yourself stuck in.

Your ideal life, without the chains of anxiety, is there for you to take. *Are you going to sit back and allow yourself to be bound to it, or are you going to act in a new way, break the cycle and achieve the life you desire?*

There's only one smart choice here.

Take the bull by the horns and go, go, go!

It's no longer acceptable to be controlled by your anxiety symptoms, especially when you know how to defeat it.

Now, remind me, what are your goals, again? Let's recap.

Chapter 20

Intentionally Reaching Goals And Changing Others

Oh Em Gee! You did it!

Congratulations! You've graduated. You've made it to the final chapter which means you've disentangled your anxiety, and you've broken free from the limitations that anxiety places on you. That is awesome, as it means you're not willing to let it take over your life!

You've made a conscious effort to move in the right direction, but it's not over for you yet. It's important that you're clear on how to reach your goals, so let's review some of the key points you've learned from this book.

Review

Take a moment to reflect on your anxiety levels when you first purchased this book. We started talking about anxiety and how it can prevent you from reaching your full potential before we clearly defined exactly what anxiety is.

- Do you understand how anxiety impacts you and prevents you from meeting your potential?

- Can you clearly define anxiety and has this helped you recognize your anxiety symptoms?

If you've answered 'yes' to both questions, that's great. This suggests your overall knowledge and understanding of anxiety has increased, which is great. Awareness is everything!

If you've answered 'no,' you may want to head back to chapters 1 and 2 to recap the information.

In Section 1, you learned about self-acceptance and explored your triggers. You also looked at how you could overcome your anxiety by researching your triggers and symptoms. They are all vital as you move into the next section of the book.

- Do you feel you have the tools and skills you need to evaluate your anxiety?
- Has your level of self-acceptance improved?
- If you are asked to identify your anxiety triggers, are you able to pinpoint some things that cause your anxiety levels to increase?
- Are you confident in researching information about your anxiety, your triggers and symptoms effectively?

If you've answered 'yes' to all these review questions, it means you're able to use this book to evaluate your anxiety.

Don't worry, you don't have to remember everything exactly, just be aware that if you're struggling to evaluate your anxiety, you can flick back to Section 1 of this book and review chapters 3-5. They will always be here for you, because anxiety doesn't mean you're alone!

In Section 2, we explored ways of managing anxiety and we focused on creating your plan of attack and taking care of your mind, body, and spirit. One important thing to come from this is that you MUST recognize how important it is to take care of yourself and doing this (even though your anxiety will make you believe you don't have time), makes a positive impact on anxiety and your life in general.

This section also talked about the benefits of planning when it comes to your anxiety, while also reflecting on ways to take time for yourself. Planning ensures you're not left in limbo, and you always know what you're doing which can be vital during times of anxiety and can improve how you manage your anxiety during the tough times. Having time to yourself can help you relax, refocus, or put things into perspective, which can make a difference on your mindset and how you process the things that have happened during your day.

Ask yourself:

- Can you formulate a plan of action to combat your anxiety symptoms?
- If new anxiety symptoms present themselves, do you feel you'll be able to evaluate them effectively (this means accepting them, to knowing your triggers, and being able to formulate a plan of action to overcome them)?
- To list three ways in which your management of your anxiety has improved.
- How do you care for your...
  - Mind?

- Body?
- Spirit?
- When your anxiety is tough, do you have plans in place to help you get through those times?
- Does this help you manage your anxiety better?
- List three benefits you've personally found by taking time to yourself.
- Are you still taking time to yourself (if not, why)?
- On a scale of 1-10 (1 being not at all, and 10 being completely), how comfortable are you putting things into perspective when it comes to your anxiety?

If you answer the above questions with ease, it means you're capable of managing your anxiety well, but it's important to remember that...

Anxiety is a journey!

Things aren't always simple when it comes to managing your anxiety and that's because everyone's experience of anxiety is different. Remember, if you're struggling with any aspect of managing your anxiety, you should refresh the chapters in Section 2, chapters 6-10.

When you've managed your anxiety well, you're ready to overcome it completely, so in Section 3, we concentrate on overcoming the most common anxieties. You've explored facing anxiety from responsibility, in relationships, when speaking, and we've also talked through anxieties that happen in everyday life and how you can prepare to overcome your anxieties, even if they are unexpected.

- Have you experienced any of the most common anxieties yourself?
- Do you think you could manage if you had to face any of the anxieties mentioned in this section?
- Do you think any of the things listed below have improved since you began leading through your anxiety...
- Your relationships?
  - Your ability to handle responsibilities?
  - Your ability to speak in public or speak out?
  - Your ability to deal with every day or unexpected anxieties that occur?

If you're answering 'yes' to most of the questions above, it means that you can overcome your anxiety, which means you can basically overcome anything that life throws at you. You've come such a long way on your journey, and in order to progress even further and head toward an anxiety-free life, the final section has some key tips to ensure you're successful, that you're beating back anxiety!

If you're not overcoming your anxieties as quickly or as well as you'd hoped, you should remember that these things take time. Take small steps, set small goals, but keep moving forward. You can always review the relevant chapters (11-14) to refresh your knowledge, should you find that some of the most common anxieties are affecting you. But remember to give yourself time!

The concluding chapters from 15-18 are filled with top tips, because even though you're managing your anxiety well, we want you to live an anxiety-free life, although you understand life is never completely anxiety-free, and that some anxiety is good. This chapter helps you stay committed to combatting your anxiety, and it explains how your own anxiety wants to deceive you. The more awareness you have of this, the easier it is to spot when your anxiety is causing you to be irrational.

This chapter also talks you through the difference between good and bad anxiety, so your clear on how to distinguish between the two and can use your anxiety to drive and motivate you. We also talk about finding relief, and how others can help you, because you no longer believe your anxious thoughts when they try to tell you that you're alone in this.

In chapter 19, you dare to dream about living your life anxiety-free, which is the ultimate goal, and you're contemplating an anxiety-free life, which is something you've probably never believed was possible, but now you believe!

- Do you understand the importance of commitment when it comes to overcoming your anxiety issues?
- Do you realize that you can't control everything when it comes to your anxiety?
- Are you able to understand how your anxiety tries to deceive you?
- Are you able to recognize when your anxiety is trying to deceive you and can you give an example of when this has happened and how you've overcome this?
- Can you think of examples when your anxiety has been a positive thing for you?

Intentionally Reaching Goals And Changing Others

- Do you think you're better at distinguishing between good anxiety and bad anxiety?
- Can you list three people or organizations who can help you get relief from your anxiety?
- Do you know who's in your support network?
- Have you dreamt about your anxiety-free life? Remind yourself what this looks like!

There's no doubt, you've made fantastic progress and are leading the way to your anxiety-free life. You've reviewed everything from knowing what anxiety is, to evaluating, managing, and overcoming your anxiety, and so much more. Now all that's left is for you to stay intentional!

Ultimately, your intention is to disentangle your anxiety, so you can learn how to identify, understand, and overcome your anxiety before it takes over your life. You're not going to let it, so stay committed, and stay intentional.

How Can I Stay Intentional When it Comes to Achieving My Goals?

When you're living an anxiety-free life, you need to stay intentional when it comes to your goals, and you must make sure your intentions are always aligned to your end goals. These often change as time passes, as you grow, but now you have the tools you need to deal with it, change is no longer scary, *right?* This means you can remain intentional when it comes to achieving your goals.

Here are 9 top tips to help you remain intentional in your life:

1. Have a clear structure for your day.

2. Be clear about your goals and priorities for the day, and also in the long term. Make sure everything aligns.
3. Ensure you plan your finances and are careful with your money (poor money management triggers anxiety).
4. Declutter your home, as clutter can trigger anxiety.
5. Manage your time well and remember to have the time you need for your family, yourself, and work.
6. Commit time to others in your life as this will strengthen the relationships in your life.
7. Cultivate and nurture a positive mindset. Don't concentrate on the negatives in life.
8. Check in with yourself and health, including your mental health. Eat healthily, exercise, relax when needed, and take time to yourself. Be aware of how your mental health is.
9. Reflect on your progress and celebrate those wins. A win means you've achieved your goals. This is an intention, so tick it off your list!

Sharing is caring, so now you know how to be more intentional, let's look at an anxiety success story—anxiety-free living is possible.

Carter the Worrier

Carter had always been a worrier, all the way through high school. When he started his first job after college, things went from bad to worse. He worried about his relationship with his girlfriend, his money, what others thought of him, but most of all, his job performance.

As a result, he struggled to sleep and found making the simplest decision difficult and time-consuming.

Enough was enough, and Carter knew this couldn't go on. He started by confiding in his girlfriend but also felt able to confide in his brother. They provided reassurance, but their advice wasn't really productive as they told him he didn't need to worry, but he couldn't help it. When his physical symptoms got too much, depression took hold and Carter decided to visit a therapist.

His therapist helped him gain a stronger understanding of his anxiety and explore the root cause of the worry. They crafted out a plan of action, which meant he practiced CBT techniques, while also practicing exposure therapy, a little at a time.

> *"For me, therapy worked much faster than I thought it would. Dealing with my fears through exposure therapy helped me accept that while anxiety was a huge part of my life, things aren't always as bad as they seem. My confidence increased as I realized I CAN deal with my anxiety, and I am worthy of my job."*
>
> *~ Carter*

Carter reports that his sleep improved, and so did his performance at work. It took a few sessions over a series of months, but he's just stepped away from his therapist and has just been told by his boss that he's in line for a promotion. Most of all, Carter comments that his relationships with his girlfriend and family members have also gone from strength to strength. They made a conscious effort to support him better and have also changed their attitude when it comes to anxiety.

Just like Carter, success is yours because you've learned the skills and knowledge needed by reading this book and now I'm holding you accountable...

You have all the tools you need to lead through anxiety, for life. Don't keep this important knowledge in your head, you need to take action and apply it to your life, so your dreams can come true.

A final word from me...

You can disentangle your anxiety.

You can overcome the symptoms.

You can have the life you desire.

You just need to act. This book alone can't make you act; this is something YOU need to do. Doing so will not only impact your own life for the better, but it will also be life-changing for those in your life too.

You're free, anxiety-free! It's kind of liberating, isn't it?

References List

Abraham, M. (2020) *Common Anxiety Triggers for Anxiety and Panic.* Calm Clinic. Available at: https://www.calmclinic.com/anxiety/causes/triggers Accessed: 10/04/2022

Abraham, M. (2020) *Here's How to Manage Anxiety.* Calm Clinic. Available at: https://www.calmclinic.com/anxiety/management Accessed: 10/19/2022

Abraham, M. (2022) *10 Ways to Stop and Calm Anxiety Quickly.* Calm Clinic. Available at: https://www.calmclinic.com/anxiety/stop-anxiety-quickly Accessed: 10/04/2022

Abramson, A. (2022) *11 Anxiety Myth'//s You Shouldn't Believe.* Minded. Available at: https://www.tryminded.com/blog/anxiety-myths Accessed: 10/01/2022

Anxiety Solutions of Denver. (no date) *Tom's Success Story.* Available at: https://www.effectivetherapysolutions.com/success-stories/success-story-tom Accessed: 11/17/2022

Azarian, B. (2016) *How Anxiety Warps Your Perception.* BBC.com. Available at: https://www.bbc.com/future/article/20160928-how-anxiety-warps-your-perception Accessed: 10/22/2022

Balance Through Simplicity. (no date) *Be Intentional: 14 Ways to be Intentional Every Day.* Available at: https://balancethroughsimplicity.com/intentional-living-and-4-easy-ways-you-can-live-with-intention-now/ Accessed: 11/20/2022

BetterHelp Editorial Team. (2022) *How to Overcome Self-Doubt and Succeed.* BetterHelp. Available at: https://www.betterhelp.com/advice/self-esteem/how-to-overcome-self-doubt-and-succeed/?utm_source=AdWords&utm_medium=Search_PPC_c&utm_term=PerformanceMax&utm_ content=&network=x&placement=&target=&matchtype=&utm_campaign=16929735023&ad_type=responsive_pmax&adposition=&gclid=Cj0KCQiA4O ybBhCzARIsAIcfn9mR1Pq_XdDANsJrtaYfBBArjd8ObTVGMxf DBM6jqxj3Q3udsSdQ8nUaAvGiEALw_wcB Accessed: 10/30/2022

Brookins, S. M. (2021) *Fear of Responsibility: Hypengyophobia.* Fearof.org. Available at: https://fearof.org/hypengyophobia/ Accessed: 10/24/2022

Cassata, C. (2019) *7 Ways to Increase Optimism and Reduce Anxiety Every Day.* Available at: https://www.healthline.com/health-news/reduce-anxiety-by-practicing-optimism-can-help#Mindful-Moves:-15-Minute-Yoga-Flow-for-Anxiety Accessed: 11/06/2022

Counselling Directory. (2015) *Self Acceptance and Anxiety.* Available at: https://www.counselling-directory.org.uk/memberarticles/self-acceptance-and-anxiety Accessed: 10/03/2022

References List

Fruitfully Alive. (no date) *How a Planner Can Help You Battle Anxiety and Depression*. Available at: https://fruitfullyalive.com/planner-can-help-battle-anxiety-depression/ Accessed: 10/18/2022

Good Reads. (2022) *Anxiety Quotes*. Available at: https://www.goodreads.com/quotes/tag/anxiety Accessed: 09/29/2022

Good Reads. (2022) *Me Time Quotes*. Available at: https://www.goodreads.com/quotes/tag/me-time Accessed: 10/20/2022

Good Reads. (2022) *Perspective Quites*. Available at: https://www.goodreads.com/quotes/tag/perspective Accessed: 10/23/2022

Greenberg, M. (2015) *9 Ways to Calm Your Anxious Mind*. Available at: https://www.psychologytoday.com/us/blog/the-mindful-self-express/201506/9-ways-calm-your-anxious-mind Accessed: 10/15/2022

Hagerty, K. (2022) *Death Anxiety: 9 Ways to Overcome Your Fear of Death*. For Hims. Available at: https://www.forhims.com/blog/death-anxiety Accessed: 10/27/2022

Heights. (2022) *The 7 Best Vitamins for Anxiety and Stress*. Available at: https://www.yourheights.com/blog/supplements/best-vitamins-for-anxiety/ Accessed: 10/15/2022

Hobson, N. (2018) *Alleviating Anxiety by Putting Things into Perspective*. Thrive Global. Available at: https://thriveglobal.com/stories/alleviating-anxiety-by-putting-things-into-perspective/ Accessed: 10/22/2022

Holland, K. (2022) *What Triggers Anxiety? 11 Causes That May Surprise You.* Healthline. Available at: https://www.healthline.com/health/anxiety/anxiety-triggers#triggers Accessed: 10/29/2022

Jovanovic, T. (no date) *What is Anxiety?* Anxiety.org. Available at: https://www.anxiety.org/what-is-anxiety Accessed: 10/03/2022

Just Mind. (2013) *Why You Should Understand Your Anxiety.* Available at: https://justmind.org/why-you-should-understand-your-anxiety/ Accessed: 10/10/2022

Kelly's Thoughts on Things. (2021) *Anxiety Triggers: Why Knowing Them is Important.* Available at: https://kellysthoughtsonthings.com/anxiety-triggers-why-knowing-them-is-important/#:~:text=Anxiety%20can%20be%20triggered%20by%20many%20different%20situations%2C,learn%20what%20circumstances%20might%20make%20your%20symptoms%20worse Accessed: 10/03/2022

Kesarovska, L. (2017) *How to Plan Your Life and Never Be Stuck Again: 5 Steps to Succeed.* Available at: https://letsreachsuccess.com/plan-your-life/ Accessed: 10/17/2022

Ladd, M. (2019) *My Anxiety Makes My Brain Feel Like a Broken Hamster Wheel.* Healthline. Available at: https://www.healthline.com/health/anxiety/signs-spinning-out-of-control#3.-Overplanning,-or-trying-to-control-the-uncontrollable- Accessed: 10/28/2022

Laughland, P. (no date) *10 Ways Helping Others Will Improve Your Life.* Lifehack. Available at: https://www.lifehack.org/

References List

articles/lifestyle/10-ways-helping-others-will-improve-your-life.html Accessed: 11/08/2022

Lowbridge, D. (no date) *How a Planner Can Help You With Anxiety Treatment at Home*. Available at: https://www.transcendingwaves.com/blogs/productivity-positivity/how-a-planner-can-help-you-with-anxiety-treatment-at-home Accessed: 10/18/2022

MantraCare. (no date) *Self Acceptance: Know About the Positive and Negative Sides*. Available at: https://mantracare.org/therapy/self-care/self-acceptance/#:~:text=Self-acceptance%20is%20the%20ability%20to%20be%20comfortable%20with,it%20leads%20to%20positive%20steps%20in%20the%20future Accessed: 10/03/2022

Mayo Clinic. (2017) *Fear of Public Speaking: How Can I Overcome it?* Available at: https://www.mayoclinic.org/diseases-conditions/specific-phobias/expert-answers/fear-of-public-speaking/faq-20058416 Accessed: 10/26/2022

Mayo Clinic. (2018) *Anxiety Disorders*. Available at: https://www.mayoclinic.org/diseases-conditions/anxiety/symptoms-causes/syc-20350961 Accessed: 09/30/2022

Mayo Clinic. (2022) *Stress Management*. Available at: https://www.mayoclinic.org/healthy-lifestyle/stress-management/in-depth/positive-thinking/art-20043950 Accessed: 10/21/2022

McGuire, J. (no date) *How to Help Someone With Anxiety*. John Hopkins Medicine. Available at: https://www.hopkinsmedicine.org/health/treatment-tests-and-therapies/how-to-help-someone-with-anxiety Accessed: 11/15/2022

MedlinePlus. (2020) *Anxiety.* National Library of Medicine. Available at: https://medlineplus.gov/anxiety.html Accessed: 10/02/2022

Mind. (2021) *Anxiety and Panic Attacks: Self-care.* Available at: https://www.mind.org.uk/information-support/types-of-mental-health-problems/anxiety-and-panic-attacks/self-care/ Accessed: 10/29/2022

Mind (2021) *Anxiety and Panic Attacks: What is Anxiety?* Available at: https://www.mind.org.uk/information-support/types-of-mental-health-problems/anxiety-and-panic-attacks/about-anxiety/?gclid=Cj0KCQiA4OybBhCzARIsAIcfn9kYLT9HeA97aMaRemWoyYIXt0-3Ovy4i1HJ0z4XcfIs_gek77SNtE4aAh_kEALw_wcB Accessed: 11/03/2022

Morin, A. (2020) *7 Tips for Finding Your Purpose in Life.* Verywellmind. Available at: https://www.verywellmind.com/tips-for-finding-your-purpose-in-life-4164689 Accessed: 10/30/2022

Nadar, J. (2019) *The Importance of Having a Good Perspective on Life.* Thrive Global. Available at: https://thriveglobal.com/stories/the-importance-of-having-a-good-perspective-on-life/ Accessed: 10/22/2022

National Center for Complementary and Integrative Health (NCCIH). (2020) *Mind and Body Approaches for Stress and Anxiety: What the Science Says.* Available at: https://www.nccih.nih.gov/health/providers/digest/mind-and-body-approaches-for-stress-science accessed: 10/15/2022

NHS.uk. (no date) *Feeling Anxious?* Available at: https://www.nhs.uk/every-mind-

References List

matters/mental-health-issues/anxiety/?WT.mc_id=Anxiety&gclid=CjwKCAjw7eSZBhB8EiwA60kCWzuhK8RJwkpEekEbeynBo0zrVOVNmSf6VANqlOfN2nN7Yas0KAVzYxoCr8QQAvD_BwE&gclsrc=aw.ds Accessed: 09/30/2022

NHS.uk. (2019) *Anxiety, Fear and Panic.* Available at: https://www.nhs.uk/mental-health/feelings-symptoms-behaviours/feelings-and-symptoms/anxiety-fear-panic/ Accessed: 11/08/2022

Organise My House. (2022) *20 Amazing Me Time Ideas for When You Need Time to Yourself.* Available at: https://organisemyhouse.com/create-some-me-time/ Accessed: 10/20/2022

Page, S. (2020) *13 Tips on How to Stay Positive During Anxious Times.* Total Wellness. Available at: https://info.totalwellnesshealth.com/blog/13-tips-on-how-to-stay-positive-during-anxious-times Accessed: 11/06/2022

Pangilinan, J. (2022) *165 Anxiety Quotes to Keep You Calm When You Feel Stressed Out.* Happier Human. Available at: https://www.happierhuman.com/anxiety-quotes/ Accessed: 11/03/2022

Parade. (2022) *101 Anxiety Quotes to Help You Get Through and Lift Your Spirits.* Available at: https://parade.com/951718/parade/anxiety-quotes/

Accessed: 10/01/2022

Park, R. (2016) *Anxiety: The Deception from the Brain.* Sandpaw. Available at: https://sandpaw.weblogs.anu.edu.au/2016/05/29/anxiety-the-deception-from-the-brain/ Accessed: 10/30/2022

Powell, A. (2022) *Relationship Anxiety: Signs, Causes & 8 Ways to Overcome.* Choosing Therapy. Available at: https://www.choosingtherapy.com/relationship-anxiety/ Accessed: 10/24/2022

PsychAlive. (2016) *How to Deal with Relationship Anxiety.* Available at: https://www.psychalive.org/how-to-deal-with-relationship-anxiety/#:~:text=It%20can%20lead%20us%20to,that%20sabotage%20our%20love%20lives Accessed: 10/26/2022

Psychology Today. (2015) *Why is it So Easy to Slip Back into Bad Habits?* Available at: https://www.psychologytoday.com/gb/blog/think-act-be/201511/why-is-it-so-easy-slip-back-bad-habits Accessed: 11/19/2022

Psych Times. (no date) *Hypengyophobia (Fear of Responsibility).* Available at: https://psychtimes.com/hypengyophobia-fear-of-responsibility/ Accessed: 10/23/2022

Raypole, C. (2019) *How to Handle Relationship Anxiety.* Healthline. Available at: https://www.healthline.com/health/relationship-anxiety#overcoming-it Accessed: 10/26/2022

Reynolds, M. (2015) *20 Questions to Plan Your Life.* Psychology Today. Available at: https://www.psychologytoday.com/us/blog/wander-woman/201512/20-questions-plan-your-life Accessed: 10/15/2022

Roberts, E. (2018) *Anxiety Decreases and Confidence Increases: How Do You Do it?* Available at: https://www.healthyplace.com/blogs/buildingselfesteem/2018/01/how-to-improve-confidence-when-you-have-anxiety#:~:text=If%20you%27re%20struggling%20with%20confidence%20

References List

and%20anxiety%2C%20then,in%20the%20world-%20that%20trigger%20doubt%20or%20fear Accessed: 10/10/2022

Schwantes, M. (2017) *9 Helpful Tips to Calm Your Nerves Before Speaking*. Inc. Available at: https://www.inc.com/marcel-schwantes/9-simple-tricks-to-overcome-your-fear-of-speaking.html Accessed: 10/27/2022

ShineSheets. (2022) *How to Use Planning to Relieve Your Anxiety*. Available at: https://www.shinesheets.com/how-to-use-planning-to-relieve-your-anxiety/ Accessed: 10/19/2022

Simple Roots Wellness. *How to Create a Battle Plan for Anxiety*. Available at: https://simplerootswellness.com/how-to-create-a-battle-plan-for-anxiety/ Accessed: 10/07/2022

Snippe, E. (2016) *101 Quotes to Inspire Speakers*. Speaker Hub. Available at: https://speakerhub.com/blog/101-quotes Accessed: 10/26/2022

Spiritual Energy Today. (2022) *Spiritual Meaning of Anxiety: Everything You Must Know*. Available at: https://spiritualenergytoday.com/spiritual-meaning-of-anxiety/ Accessed: 10/13/2022

Spiritualify. (2019) *10 Ways to Increase Your Spiritual Power and Unleash Your Maximum Potential* Available at: https://blog.spiritualify.com/10-ways-to-increase-your-spiritual-power-and-unleash-your-maximum-potential/ accessed: 10/13/2022

Star, K. (2020) *The Benefits of Anxiety and Nervousness*. Very Well Mind. Available at: https://www.verywellmind.com/

benefits-of-anxiety-2584134#:~:text=People%20who%20have%20dealt%20with,are%20dealing%20with%20personal%20challenges Accessed: 10/01/2022

Sturken, S. (2016) *Why Perspective is Important.* Odyssey. Available at: https://www.theodysseyonline.com/why-perspective-important Accessed: 10/22/2022

Sutton, J. (2019) *The Benefits of Mental Health According to Science.* Positive Psychology. Available at: https://positivepsychology.com/benefits-of-mental-health/#:~:text=Other%20benefits%20of%20mental%20health%20include%2C%20but%20aren%E2%80%99t,Reduced%20risk%20of%20depression.%207%20Improvements%20in%20relationships Accessed: 10/15/2022

The House of Wellness. (2018) *The Importance of Me Time.* Available at: https://www.houseofwellness.com.au/wellbeing/mental-wellness/importance-of-me-time Accessed: 10/20/2022

Tye, K. (2016) *7 Ways Anxiety Actually Works to Your Advantage.* GoodTherapy. Available at: https://www.goodtherapy.org/blog/7-ways-anxiety-actually-works-to-your-advantage-0202165 Accessed: 11/02/2011

Universal Storyteller. (2019) *Avoiding Responsibility Means Giving Up the Power to Grow.* Available at: https://universalstory.medium.com/avoiding-responsibility-means-giving-up-the-power-to-grow-3f6ee09bfe8f Accessed: 10/24/2022

Vukelich, L. (2022) *Anxiety Triggers You Should Know About.* CNET. Available at: https://www.cnet.com/

References List

health/mental/10-common-anxiety-triggers/ Accessed: 03/10/2022

Whitworth, E. (2021) *Avoiding Responsibility: How it Harms Mental Health.* Shortform. Available at: https://www.shortform.com/blog/avoiding-responsibility/ Accessed: 10/24/2022

Wooll, M. (2002) *The Secret to Finding Your Passion isn't Looking, it's Doing.* BetterUp. Available at: https://www.betterup.com/blog/how-to-find-your-passion Accessed: 11/01/2022

Wyeth, S. (2014). *17 Inspiring Quotes to Help You Face Your Fears.* Inc. Available at: https://www.inc.com/sims-wyeth/17-inspiring-quotes-to-help-you-face-your-fears.html Accessed: 10/24/2022

Printed in Great Britain
by Amazon